cucina
essenziale
ESSENTIAL
COOKING

stefano cavallini

Dedicated to my family
and my love Laura

RECIPE NOTES

All recipes serve 4
All eggs are size A
All olive oil is extra virgin
All pepper is white – this is to avoid black
flecks in pale sauces, dressings and soups.
All sugar is caster sugar
All lemons are unwaxed
All flour is plain flour, type 00 or type 0
Vegetables and fruit are medium unless
otherwise stated
1 tbsp = 15ml/ ^{1}/2 fl oz

First published
in Great Britain in 2000 by
PAVILION BOOKS LIMITED
London House, Great Eastern Wharf
Parkgate Road, London SW11 4NQ

Text © Stefano Cavallini
Photography © David Brittain
Design and layout
© Pavilion Books Ltd.

The moral right of the author and
photographer has been asserted.

Design and Art direction
by Stafford Cliff

Production artwork by
Matt Sarraf

Product styling by
Sarita Sharma

A CIP catalogue record for this book is
available from the British Library.

ISBN 1 86205 3979

Set in Monaco
Printed in Singapore
by Imago
Colour reproduction by Alliance Graphics

2 4 6 8 10 9 7 5 3 1

This book can be ordered
direct from the publisher.
Please contact the Marketing Department.
But try your bookshop first.

Contents

Genius and transgression

FOREWORD BY ANDREA PINI, HEAD CHEF AT PRIMI BACI, TOKYO

Some moments in our existence stay vivid for ever. Such moments are often related to people who enter our life and influence its path. Stefano Cavallini is one of those people. I can still picture myself with Stefano and other mutual friends on a summer evening in 1991, toasting Stefano's departure for London. Leaving Lugo, his native Romagnolo town, he was going to London to become head chef for Gualtiero Marchesi at the restaurant at the Halkin Hotel, a small but exclusive hotel in the heart of Belgravia. On that very occasion Stefano asked me to go with him. I accepted at once. That evening and that choice changed my life both professionally and personally. My friendship with Stefano developed in London into a fascinating relationship, and in that city I also met a wonderful woman who is now my wife. At the Halkin, Stefano was for me not only a model professional who improved my cooking, but also an expert on gastronomy – most unusual for a man of only 24, as Stefano was then. To describe Stefano Cavallini in a few words is a hard task, especially for someone who has known him a long time. Perhaps the celebrated chef Marco Pierre White has described him better than anybody: 'He's probably as crackers as I am.' Stefano is in fact a transgressive genius. He is creative in his unpredictability, and has just the right measure of extravagance, but his cooking transcends all ordinary definitions of genius.

At work Stefano is meticulous and scrupulous to the point of exasperation. He aims constantly at perfection: from the freshness of raw materials to the final execution of the dish; from the impeccable organisation of the kitchen to the relationship with his colleagues, which is based on mutual respect. Stefano inherited from Marchesi an intellectual curiosity and complete openness towards the world of cooking. The first quality has enabled him to improve himself continuously; the second quality freed him from old prejudices and allowed him to be inspired by gastronomic models and cultures apparently far from ours. What Stefano seeks is balance without excesses, and without distorting the great traditions and enormous potential of Italian cooking. Under Marchesi's tutelage, and then independently, Stefano brought the Halkin restaurant to European recognition, and he has established himself as one of the best Italian chefs of the past generation.

Cucina Essenziale is testament to Stefano as both a supreme executor of Marchesi's cooking style, and as a creative, independent interpreter of the concept of essential cooking. The book is rooted in the past, but also represents the realisation of ambitions that Stefano cherished from the first months of our London adventure. I am happy to have shared such feelings with him, and to have been there during his first steps at the Halkin restaurant. I am happy to have been there for the first disillusion, which was followed by years of success and happiness (how many bottles of champagne we opened in our apartment!). I am happy to have shared in London evenings that lasted until dawn, in mutual friends, and even in frustrations (we once flew to Paris to have lunch at Robuchon but could not find a table despite having booked three months earlier).

Many years have passed, and although our professional paths have parted our friendship and mutual esteem remain undiminished. To go back to London and meet Stefano, who is generous, available, always full of ideas and projects, and has a new wisdom with the passing years is, for me, always a pleasure. I am constantly surprised by the quality of his cooking, by his talent and by his tastes that have not changed over time. My sincerest wish, a wish that comes from an old friend, is that his exceptional qualities will not change even when success and fame, which he fully deserves, make him even more visible to the eyes of a larger audience. To use an old Italian wish for good fortune, 'in bocca al lupo', Stefano!

La cucina essenziale

La cucina essenziale is derived from research into ancient Italian culinary traditions reinterpreted in the light of today's taste and way of life. Whereas in the past food represented the principal source of energy and had to be both plentiful and rich, nowadays we have a more discriminating sense of the immediate delights and essence of eating.

Cucina Essenziale aims to provide a balanced menu through the well-considered combination of ingredients. It aims to be light by replacing heavy sauces, fats and cream with vegetable broth, olive oil and other more suitable elements. It uses cooking techniques chosen to preserve the nutrients and to emphasize the essence of each individual ingredient.

It aims to be simple in presentation, each dish seeking to reveal the spirit of its creator without any superfluous gesture.

Tutto questo perché?
Perché a tutto c'é un perché!

11

Introduction

STEFANO CAVALLINI

La cucina essenziale is the name for the style of cooking that I have been perfecting ever since I came to London. It is not typical Italian cooking, but a refined cuisine that happens to be practised by Italians. The basics were taught to me in Milan by the Grand Maestro, Gualtiero Marchesi. From him I learnt a passion for food as well as how to work with it without compromising on flavour. It's true that one can learn the techniques of cooking only from studying, from apprenticeships and from travelling, but the stimulus to cook and to succeed comes from the people with whom you work, and who believe in what you're doing.

Ten years ago I arrived in London to work as head chef for Gualtiero Marchesi, who was the consultant at the Halkin Hotel at that time. The first few months were very difficult, above all because I did not speak the language. At this time I had support from two people in particular: Richard Stuart, sous-chef, and Besa Bruno, perhaps the greatest sommelier of Italian wines and now an importer of wines into Britain. But it was Marchesi who kept me going in the face of initial scepticism from the public. They reacted with shock; at that time only Penati, of Harry's Bar, was cooking great Italian food. For the rest it was Italian tradition reduced to its barest bones: lasagne, overcooked spaghetti, and pizza.

The first few reviews criticised everything: the pasta was too 'al dente', the meat too pink, the risotto spread out on a flat plate rather than being heaped up in a bowl. In short, for an unsuspecting public it was too much too soon. So I am very grateful to all the people who supported me through that period, especially Marchesi, of course, and the general manager of the Halkin, Mr Rettie, who allowed me to continue doing what I believed in.

In 1993 Marchesi ended his period of consultancy at the Halkin and I left for Mallorca. Yet after four months I returned to London because I wanted to finish what I had started.

Three years passed and other great Italian chefs opened restaurants of high quality. More and more Italian products were starting to appear on the market (their French equivalents had long been available). I decided that the time was ripe to start building up a proper kitchen brigade and to show just what *la cucina essenziale* stood for. In 1995 I won the first Michelin star ever to be awarded to an Italian restaurant in England. I was overjoyed, but it was all down to Marchesi, who taught me to follow my own instincts and not to cook for the crowd. In 1997 the Halkin restaurant was renamed Stefano Cavallini and, under the guidance of Mauro Governato, director of the restaurant, things have gone from strength to strength ever since.

The restaurant scene in London has changed since those early days. Now ninety per cent of restaurants serve risotto as we do at the Halkin and the newspapers describe it as the best in London. But *la cucina essenziale* continues to develop; every day it gets better, more focused and true to itself. I'm proud to say, for example, that ninety per cent of the sauces I use are vegetable sauces and are, as you will see, an important starting point for many of my recipes.

I could not have produced this book without the help of some key people: Mirco Rocca, head chef at the Halkin; Michela Battasso, head chef of I Sapori di Stefano Cavallini; Jorg Wolf, pastry chef; Massimiliano Folli, who chose all the wines for the recipes; and, of course, the rest of the kitchen brigade. My special thanks go to Charlotte Coleman-Smith, the cookery writer, who worked tirelessly with me on my recipes and text ensuring that the recipes are fully accessible to the home cook. This book is an attempt to distil my spirit and that which emanates from my colleagues in the kitchen every day. I hope that everyone who reads it – the domestic cook, the lay reader, the professional chef – will be inspired to try my recipes. I wish them good luck and good cooking.

Basic recipes

STOCKS

A good homemade stock is essential for providing depth of flavour to a dish. Stocks are not difficult to make, and if you are keen to get the most out of your cooking it's well worth preparing some to freeze ahead of time in small quantities; remember to label the containers so that you know how much to unfreeze. Most stocks will keep in the fridge for two to three days, or for up to three months in the freezer. Adding ice to a meat or fish stock causes the pores in the bones to close slightly. As the stock heats up, the flavours are released slowly, along with any impurities - these can be skimmed off the surface as the stock simmers. Aim to use approximately equal volumes of water and ice.

COURT-BOUILLON

Court-bouillon is a light stock, often used for poaching or steaming food. In the restaurant I often steam pieces of meat instead of cooking them in the oven. This keeps them beautifully tender. Depending on what you are steaming and on your tastes, you can change the ingredients accordingly. If I use a court-bouillon to steam lamb, for example, I use lots of white pepper - this gives the meat a wonderful flavour without it being too overwhelming. This recipe is very easy to prepare, so I recommend you make it fresh every time you need it.

Makes about 3.2 l/5$\frac{1}{2}$ pints

1 onion, about 150 g/5$\frac{1}{2}$ oz, roughly chopped
1 carrot, about 150 g/5$\frac{1}{2}$ oz, roughly chopped
1 celery stick, about 100 g/3$\frac{1}{2}$ oz, roughly chopped
1 leek, about 100 g/5$\frac{1}{2}$ oz, roughly chopped
1 lemon, quartered
4 bay leaves
pinch of white pepper
3 parsley sprigs
3 l/5$\frac{1}{4}$ pints water
200 ml/8 fl oz white wine

Put the vegetables into a large pan with the lemon. Add the bay leaves, white pepper, parsley, water and wine. Bring to the boil. The court-bouillon is now ready to use.

BRODO DI PESCE Fish stock

It's best to use the bones from white fish such as turbot, John Dory, sea bass or Dover sole for this recipe. Your fishmonger should be able to sell you these.

Makes about 1.5 l/2$\frac{3}{4}$ pints

1 whole head of garlic, unpeeled
1 tbsp olive oil
1 onion, about 150 g/5$\frac{1}{2}$ oz, roughly chopped
3 celery stalks, about 300 g/10$\frac{1}{2}$ oz, roughly chopped
1 leek, about 100 g/3$\frac{1}{2}$ oz, roughly chopped
1 fennel bulb, about 100 g/3$\frac{1}{2}$ oz, roughly chopped
3 bay leaves
pinch of white pepper
3 parsley sprigs
800 g/1lb 12 oz white fish bones
1 tbsp Pernod or Martini Vermouth
3 tbsp white wine
cold water, to cover (about 1.5 l/2$\frac{3}{4}$ pints)
ice cubes, to cover

Peel the tough outer skin from the garlic head, then cut the head in half - you don't need to peel or separate the cloves. In a stockpot or large pan heat the olive oil, then add the garlic, chopped vegetables, bay leaves, white pepper and parsley and cook for 5 minutes over a medium heat until the vegetables are soft but not browned. Add the fish bones and cook for another 8-10 minutes, then add the Martini and white wine and cook for 5 minutes. Add enough water and ice cubes to cover the contents of the pan. Bring the liquid slowly to the boil, then lower the heat and simmer very gently for about 30 minutes, skimming the surface regularly. Remove the stock from the heat and skim the surface once more. Leave to rest for 20 minutes before straining through a chinois or fine-meshed sieve lined with muslin. Allow to cool, then refrigerate or freeze until needed.

BRODO DI CROSTACEI Shellfish stock

Makes about 150ml/$\frac{1}{4}$ pint

2 kg/4$\frac{1}{2}$ lb crayfish heads, shells and claws; or lobster shells; or crab shells
2 carrots, cut into cubes
1 celery stick, cut into cubes
$\frac{1}{2}$ leek, cubed
$\frac{1}{2}$ onion, cubed
$\frac{1}{2}$ head garlic
1 tomato, roughly chopped
2 bay leaves
pinch of white pepper
100 ml/3$\frac{1}{2}$ fl oz brandy
100 ml/3$\frac{1}{2}$ fl oz white wine
cold water, to cover (about 2 l/3$\frac{1}{2}$ pints)
ice cubes, to cover

Preheat the oven to 180°C/350°F/gas mark 4. Place the heads, shells and claws in an ovenproof pan, place in the oven and roast for 10 minutes. Remove from the oven and add the carrots, celery, leek, onion, garlic, tomato, bay leaves and white pepper. Pour the brandy over the vegetables and shells, then flame the brandy by carefully lighting the surface with a match, keeping well back as you do so. Pour over the wine and simmer over a medium heat until the liquid has reduced by half, then add enough ice and cold water to cover the contents of the pan. Slowly bring the liquid to the boil and simmer for 40-50 minutes, skimming constantly. Strain into a clean pan and heat until reduced by half. Pass through a chinois or fine-meshed sieve lined with muslin. Allow to cool, then refrigerate or freeze until needed.

BRODO DI POLLO Chicken stock

A hen or *gallina* is the female, egg-laying chicken; the male chicken is called the *pollo*, and is the one used for roasting. After a couple of years of egg-laying the hen is often used as the basis for a stock; its tougher meat means it can be cooked for much longer, and it produces a good flavour. You may need to order your boiling fowl from your butcher in advance as many shops no longer stock them as a matter of course. If you can't find one, you could substitute an ordinary large chicken. Your butcher should be able to sell you chicken joints. You can also find them frozen in packs but defrost them thoroughly before use.

Makes about 3 l/5¼ pints

1 kg/2¼ lb raw chicken carcasses or joints
1 boiling fowl, about 2.5 kg/5½ lb
1 onion, about 150 g/5½ oz, roughly chopped
1 carrot, about 150 g/5½ oz, roughly chopped
3 celery stalks, about 150 g/5½ oz, roughly chopped
1 leek, about 100 g/3½ oz, roughly chopped
cold water, to cover (about 3 l/5¼ pints)
ice cubes, to cover

Put the chicken carcasses, the fowl and the vegetables in a stockpot or large pan. Add enough water and ice to cover the contents of the pan. Bring to the boil, then lower the heat and simmer very gently for about 3 hours, skimming the surface regularly. Remove the stock from the heat and skim the surface once more. Leave to settle for 20 minutes before straining through a chinois or fine-meshed sieve lined with muslin. Allow to cool, then refrigerate or freeze until needed.

BRODO DI CONIGLIO Rabbit stock

Follow the method for chicken stock, replacing the chicken carcasses with an equivalent weight of rabbit bones and omitting the fowl. Simmer for 1 hour instead of 3.

BRODO VEGETALE Vegetable stock

This is a good basic stock for every kitchen, and one that I use frequently in this book. It can be used as an alternative to court-bouillon when steaming food with very delicate flavours.

Makes about 1.5 l/2¾ pints

1 onion, about 150 g/5½ oz, roughly chopped
1 carrot, about 150 g/5½ oz, roughly chopped
3 celery stalks, about 100 g/3½ oz, roughly chopped
1 leek, about 100 g/3½ oz, roughly chopped
1 fennel bulb, about 200 g/7 oz, roughly chopped
2 courgettes, about 300 g/10½ oz, roughly chopped
1 aubergine, about 200 g/7oz, roughly chopped
3 parsley sprigs
cold water, to cover (about 3 l/5¼ pints)

Place the chopped vegetables and parsley in a stockpot or large pan. Add cold water to cover, then bring slowly to the boil. Lower the heat and simmer very gently for 2 hours, skimming the surface regularly. Remove the pan from the heat, skim the surface once more and strain immediately through a chinois or fine-meshed sieve lined with muslin. Allow to cool, then refrigerate or freeze until the stock is needed.

JUS

Many of my recipes call for jus: this is a concentrated reduced stock that is used in sauce-making. In a restaurant kitchen chefs will make a jus specifically for a recipe - partridge jus for a partridge dish, rabbit jus for a rabbit recipe, and so on. However, when cooking at home you can restrict yourself to either veal or chicken jus. If you want to make a specific jus, simply follow the method for the veal jus, varying it as described below. Store in the fridge for up to two days, and in the freezer for up to three months.

FONDO DI POLLO/FONDO DI QUAGLIA/FONDO DI PICCIONE

Chicken jus/Quail jus/Pigeon jus
Follow the method for veal jus, below, replacing the veal ribs with chicken, quail or pigeon carcasses and bones.

FONDO DI CAPRIOLO Venison jus
Follow the method for veal jus, adding juniper berries.

FONDO DI ANATRA Duck jus
Follow the method for veal jus, adding 100 ml/3½ fl oz soy sauce.

FONDO DI AGNELLO Lamb jus
Follow the method for veal jus, omitting the onion, carrot, celery and leek.

FONDO DI VITELLO Veal jus
This is an extremely useful jus and one that we use frequently in the restaurant. Along with chicken jus, it forms the base of countless sauces. Your butcher should be able to supply you with veal ribs. Ask him to cut them up if they are large, and try to obtain some shin bones as well. As this jus is so concentrated, you need to start off with large quantities of bones and water to make a relatively small amount of jus. Don't chop the vegetables too finely or they will turn into purée. If you are using small carrots, for example, you could leave them whole.

Makes 500 ml/9 fl oz

5 kg/11 lb veal ribs
1 whole head of garlic, unpeeled
cold water, to cover (about 5 l/8¾ pints)
ice, to cover
1 onion, about 200 g/7 oz, roughly chopped
1 carrot, about 150 g/5½ oz, roughly chopped
2 celery stalks, about 150 g/5½ oz, roughly chopped
1 leek, about 200 g/7 oz, roughly chopped
2 tomatoes, deseeded and roughly chopped
2 thyme sprigs
3 bay leaves
2 rosemary sprigs
1 tsp tomato purée

Preheat the oven to 180°C/350°F/gas mark 4. Place the veal ribs in cast-iron roasting pans and roast in the oven for 20 minutes or until browned, turning them occasionally. Do this in batches if necessary. Remove from the oven and, using a teaspoon, scrape away the bone marrow from the back of the ribs; this stops the stock from going cloudy.
Peel the tough outer skin from the garlic and chop the head in half.
Put the roasted ribs in a large stockpot, add enough water and ice cubes to cover the ribs and bring to the boil. Lower the heat and add the garlic, vegetables, tomatoes, herbs and tomato purée. Skim the surface to remove any impurities and simmer very gently for about 2 hours. Strain the stock into a second, clean pan and simmer again until reduced by half. Strain through a chinois or fine-meshed sieve lined with muslin, allow to cool, then refrigerate or freeze until needed.

SAUCES

PESTO Pesto sauce
This will keep in a sealed container in the fridge for one week, or in the freezer for two months. If you decide to freeze it, don't add the Parmesan until it has defrosted thoroughly and you're ready to serve. If you like, you can use 20 g/½ oz pine nuts instead of a mixture of pine nuts and walnuts.

Makes 250 g/9 oz

10 g/¼ oz pine nuts
10 g/¼ oz walnuts
25 g/1 oz grated Parmesan
100 g/3½ oz basil leaves
100 ml/3½ fl oz olive oil
salt and white pepper

Place the pine nuts, walnuts and Parmesan in a food processor or liquidizer and process until smooth. With the motor still running, add the basil leaves, then slowly add the oil. Blend again until smooth. Season to taste. Alternatively, put the basil leaves in a pestle and mortar with the pine nuts and walnuts. Grind to a smooth paste, then gradually add the Parmesan and the olive oil. Pass the paste through a chinois or fine-meshed sieve. Season to taste.
Serve with freshly cooked pasta.

VEGETABLE SAUCES
Vegetable sauces are key components in my cooking, essential accessories that enhance and complement fish, meat and poultry dishes. They rely, quite simply, on the intrinsic flavour and natural colour of the vegetable. They are fantastically simple to prepare and endlessly adaptable. Most of the sauces given here can be served as soups, for example - just vary the amount of stock to achieve the consistency you prefer. They can also be used as pasta sauces. Of course, it's vital to use a good stock that can carry the flavour of the vegetable without either overwhelming or underplaying it. You can store vegetable

sauces in the fridge for four or five days, but they will begin to lose flavour and colour after day one. Only whisk in the final emulsifying olive oil just before serving.

SALSA DI CARCIOFI Artichoke sauce
This sauce is excellent served with fish and pasta.

Makes 600-700 ml/1-1¼ pints

5 globe artichokes, about 500 g/1 lb 2 oz
juice of 2 lemons
2 tbsp olive oil
2 garlic cloves, crushed
2 thyme sprigs
salt and white pepper
2 tbsp dry white wine

Peel off the tough outer leaves of each artichoke and reserve to make a stock. Wash the leaves carefully, then put them in a pan filled with 1 l/1¾ pints cold water. Bring to the boil, then reduce the heat and simmer for 20 minutes. Remove from the heat and leave to stand for another 30 minutes.
Prepare a bowl of acidulated water (water with lemon juice). Once you have reached the tender heart of each artichoke, cut off the top third and scoop out the choke with a teaspoon. Slice off a small amount of the green stalk at the bottom and slice the artichoke into pieces. Place the pieces in the water to stop them from turning brown.
In a large pan heat the oil, then add the crushed garlic and thyme. Drain the sliced artichoke, add to the pan, season and sauté for about 5 minutes. Pour the wine into the pan and leave to evaporate. Strain the artichoke stock, season to taste, then add to the pan and bring to the boil. Simmer gently for 20-30 minutes until the artichokes are tender. Strain the artichokes, reserving the cooking liquid but discarding the garlic. Place the artichokes in a blender with some of the cooking liquid and pulse to a purée, adding more liquid as required. Pass through a chinois or fine-meshed sieve. Season to taste and, if serving immediately, whisk in 1 tbsp olive oil to finish.

SALSA DI ASPARAGI Asparagus sauce

Makes 600 ml/1 pint

600 g/1lb 5 oz asparagus stalks
salt and white pepper
2 tbsp olive oil
1 shallot, finely chopped
1 garlic clove, crushed
500 ml/18 fl oz vegetable stock

Prepare a bowl of iced water. Trim the woody end of the asparagus and discard the trimmings. Cut the asparagus into pieces and blanch in plenty of boiling salted water for about 3 minutes. Refresh in the iced water and drain. Heat 1 tbsp olive oil in a pan and add the shallot and garlic. Heat the vegetable stock in a separate pan. When the garlic and shallot start to colour, add the asparagus, season and sauté for about 5 minutes. Add the hot vegetable stock and leave to simmer for 10 minutes - don't cook the asparagus for longer than this or it will lose colour. Strain the asparagus, reserving the liquid but discarding the garlic. Place the asparagus in a blender with some of the cooking liquid and pulse to a purée, adding more liquid as required. Pass through a chinois or fine-meshed sieve. Season to taste and, if serving immediately, whisk in 1 tbsp olive oil to finish.

SALSA DI PISELLI Pea sauce
This is particularly delicious served with pigeon, but is also good with fish or pasta, or served as a soup. In the restaurant we always use fresh peas. However, you can use frozen if fresh are unavailable. You will have a much smoother sauce if you skin the peas, but if you find the prospect daunting, leave the skins on.

Makes 600-700 ml/1-1¼ pints

450 g/1 lb fresh or frozen peas
salt and white pepper
2 tbsp olive oil
1 shallot, about 50 g/2 oz, finely chopped
35 g/1¼ oz Parma ham, sliced into fine strips
500 ml/18 fl oz vegetable stock

Prepare a bowl of iced water. Skin the peas, then blanch them in boiling salted water for about 3 minutes. Refresh in the iced water, then drain. In a large pan heat 1 tbsp olive oil, then add the shallot and Parma ham. When the shallot begins to colour, add the peas and seasoning and sauté for 5 minutes over a medium heat. Heat the stock in a separate pan, add it to the peas to cover, and simmer gently for a further 10 minutes. Don't cook the peas for longer than this or they will lose colour.

Strain the peas, reserving the liquid. Place the peas in a blender with some of the cooking liquid and pulse to a purée, adding more liquid as required. Pass through a chinois or fine-meshed sieve. Season to taste and, if serving immediately, whisk in 1 tbsp olive oil to finish.

SALSA DI CAVOLFIORI Cauliflower sauce
This sauce is good served with all types of meat, and is excellent with pheasant.

Makes 600-700 ml/1-1¼ pints

500 g/1 lb 2 oz cauliflower, cut into florets
salt and white pepper
2 tbsp olive oil
50 g/1¾ oz onion, finely chopped
2 garlic cloves, crushed
500 ml/18 fl oz vegetable stock

Prepare a bowl of iced water. Blanch the cauliflower florets in plenty of boiling salted water for 8 minutes. Transfer immediately to the iced water, then drain. In a large pan heat 1 tbsp olive oil, add the onion and garlic and, once they have begun to colour, add the cauliflower. Season and sauté for 5 minutes over a medium heat. Heat the stock in a separate pan, then add to the cauliflower. Simmer gently for a further 15-20 minutes. Strain the cauliflower, reserving the liquid but discarding the garlic. Place the cauliflower in a blender with some of the cooking liquid and pulse to a purée, adding more liquid as required. Pass through a chinois or fine-meshed sieve. Season to taste and, if serving immediately, whisk in 1 tbsp olive oil to finish.

SALSA DI BROCCOLI Broccoli sauce
This sauce is particularly good with fish and shellfish.

Makes 600-700 ml/1-1¼ pints

500 g/1 lb 2 oz broccoli, cut into florets
salt and white pepper
3 anchovies
1 tsp capers
1 garlic clove
½ small red chilli, deseeded
1 shallot, finely chopped
2 tbsp olive oil
500 ml/18 fl oz vegetable stock

Prepare a bowl of iced water. Blanch the broccoli in plenty of boiling salted water for 3 minutes. Refresh in the iced water, then drain. Finely chop the anchovies, capers, garlic, chilli and shallots together in a food processor or by hand.
In a large pan heat 1 tbsp olive oil, add the chopped ingredients and fry gently for 10 minutes. Add the broccoli to the anchovy mixture and season to taste. Heat the stock in a separate pan. Add the hot stock to the broccoli and simmer gently for 8-10 minutes. Don't overcook or the sauce will lose its bright colour.
Strain the mixture, reserving the liquid. Transfer the mixture to a blender with some of the cooking liquid and pulse briefly to a purée, adding more liquid as required. Pass through a chinois or fine-meshed sieve. Season to taste and, if serving immediately, whisk in 1 tbsp olive oil to finish.

SALSA DI CAVOLO NERO Cavolo Nero sauce
This sauce goes well with game, or with strong-tasting fish such as John Dory.

Makes 600-700 ml/1-1¼ pints

600 g/1 lb 5 oz cavolo nero
salt and white pepper
2 tbsp olive oil
50 g/1¾ oz shallots, finely chopped
2 garlic cloves, crushed
100 g/3½ oz potatoes, peeled and finely diced
500 ml/18 fl oz vegetable stock

Prepare a bowl of iced water. Remove the tough central stalk from each cavolo nero leaf by slicing it out with a knife. Blanch the leaves in plenty of boiling salted water for 5 minutes. Refresh in the iced water and drain well.
In a large pan heat 1 tbsp olive oil, add the shallots and garlic and once they begin to colour add the cavolo nero leaves and diced potatoes. Season to taste and sauté for 5 minutes. Heat the stock in a separate pan. Add the stock to the cavolo nero and potatoes and simmer gently for 10-15 minutes. Be careful not to overcook or the leaves will lose colour.
Strain the cavolo nero, reserving the liquid but discarding the garlic. Transfer the leaves to a blender with some of the cooking liquid and pulse to a purée, adding more liquid as required. Pass through a chinois or fine-meshed sieve. Season to taste and, if serving immediately, whisk in 1 tbsp olive oil to finish.

SALSA VINO ROSSO Red wine sauce

This is a classic sauce that is excellent served with either meat or fish. Use a red wine with a high tannin content for best results. The sauce will keep for one week in the fridge, but I don't advise freezing it as it will lose flavour.

Makes 300-400 ml/10-14 fl oz

1.5 l/2³/₄ pints red wine
3 shallots, finely chopped
500 ml/18 fl oz port
250 ml/9 fl oz veal jus (see page 18)
20 g/³/₄ oz butter, to serve
salt and white pepper, to serve

Pour the wine into a large pan with the shallots and bring to the boil. Light the surface with a match - standing well back as you do - and leave for a few seconds before blowing out the flame (this burns off the alcohol). Simmer until reduced by one-third, then add the port. Bring to the boil again and 'flame' as before. Simmer to reduce by half, add the veal jus and simmer until reduced by half again. Strain and, if you are serving immediately, whisk in the butter (this makes the sauce glossy) and season to taste. Otherwise, omit the seasoning and butter, allow to cool, and refrigerate until needed.

SALSA AGRODOLCE Sweet-and-sour sauce

This sauce sounds typically Chinese but in fact, it is also very common in the south of Italy. I like to serve it with deep-fried vegetables or fish. If you serve it with fish, add 1 tbsp fish stock for every 50 ml/2 fl oz sauce, but don't add the stock until you are ready to serve. The sauce will keep for up to one month in a sealed container in the store cupboard.

Makes about 500 ml/18 fl oz

600 g/1 lb 5 oz sugar
1 l/1³/₄ pints white wine vinegar

Put the sugar in a large heavy-based pan and pour in 250 ml/9 fl oz vinegar. Bring slowly to the boil, stirring constantly to dissolve the sugar. Add the remaining vinegar, lower the heat and simmer gently for 10 minutes until reduced by two-thirds. Use immediately, or allow to cool and store in a sealed glass container.

BURRO ACIDO Acid butter

I use acid butter to give flavour to my risotti - I love the extra sharpness the butter adds to the rice. This will keep for up to one week in the fridge.

Makes 600 g/1 lb 5 oz

700 ml/1¹/₄ pints dry white wine
250 ml/9 fl oz white wine vinegar
2 onions (about 200 g/7 oz), roughly chopped
500 g/1 lb 2 oz butter, diced

Pour the white wine and vinegar into a large pan and add the onions. Bring to the boil and simmer for 20 minutes until the liquid has reduced to one-tenth of its original volume. Remove from the heat and add the butter, stirring well. When all the butter has melted, pass the liquid through a chinois or fine-meshed sieve into a heatproof bowl. Allow to cool and store, covered, in the fridge until needed.

masterclass 1: puff pastry
pasta sfoglia

Makes 1.25 kg/2³/₄ lb

500 g/1 lb 2 oz
strong flour
(type 0), plus
50 g/1³/₄ oz for
the butter block

35 g/1¹/₄ oz
caster sugar

15 g/¹/₂ oz salt

3 egg yolks

200 ml/7 fl oz
ice-cold water

450 g/1 lb butter,
chilled and cut
into small pieces

Puff pastry is made by putting butter between sheets of pastry, then repeatedly rolling and folding to build up layers. It does take some time to make but it's well worth the effort and can be a satisfying way to spend an afternoon. Make sure that your environment is as cool as possible and that the butter is well chilled. Put it in the fridge wrapped in foil for 30 minutes if it is not hard enough.

1 Sift the flour, sugar and salt into a bowl and make a well in the centre. Mix the egg yolks and water together and pour these into the well. Work the liquid into the dry ingredients and knead together gently until you have formed a soft dough. Avoid overworking the dough and be careful not to add too much flour or the dough will become glutinous and rubbery. Cover tightly with clingfilm, make a cross on the top with a knife and chill for 30 minutes in the fridge.

2 To make the butter block, place the butter with 50 g/1¾ oz flour in a mixing bowl and gently 'squeeze' the butter into the flour until it is well mixed. Pat into a ball.

3 Place the butter mixture on a sheet of greaseproof paper, cover it with another sheet of paper and roll into a 15 x 20 cm/6 x 8 in rectangle about 2 cm/¾ in thick. Chill in the fridge for 20 minutes until firm. The butter block should not be so soft that it is hard to handle and should not be so firm that it cracks or breaks if you press on it. Ideally, the dough and the butter block should have the same consistency.

4 Remove the dough from the fridge and pull out the corners of the cuts you made previously to make a square shape. On a lightly floured surface roll out the dough into a square slightly thicker in the centre than at the sides, and slightly larger than the butter block, turning it as you roll.

5 Place the butter block diagonally within the square so there are four triangles around the sides. Fold these dough triangles up and over the butter block to meet in the centre like an envelope so the butter is covered.

Try to leave a slight air gap between the dough and the sides of the butter. Pinch the edges together to seal in the butter block.

6 Now roll out the folded dough on a large worksurface into a rectangle 30 x 10 cm/12 x 4 in, pressing evenly and lightly so as not to squeeze out the butter.

7 Position the dough with the long side closest to you. Make a vertical mark in the centre of the rectangle. Fold each end of the dough inwards to meet at this mark.

Brush away any excess flour from the top of the dough and fold the right-hand side inwards once more as if you were closing a book.

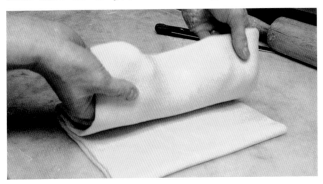

The dough has now undergone 1 double turn. Carefully place the dough on a baking sheet, cover with clingfilm and refrigerate for 30 minutes.

8 Remove the dough from the fridge and place it in front of you so that the short ends of the rectangle face to your left and right, opposite from the way the dough lay when you 'closed the book' with the first turn.

9 Repeat steps 6, 7 and 8 three more times to give the dough 4 double turns in total. Refrigerate it each time, between each turn.

10 This pastry will keep in the fridge for up to 4 days, or in the freezer for several months. When you take it out of the freezer, put it in the fridge to defrost thoroughly before using.

Starters

I

Scaloppa di fegato grasso al vapore, insalata di fave e piselli

STEAMED FOIE GRAS WITH SALAD OF BROAD BEANS AND PEAS

125 g/4½ oz
broad beans

125 g/4½ oz peas

about 1½ pints
court-bouillon
(see page 16)

4 fresh foie gras
slices, about
125 g/4½ oz each

1 tbsp olive oil

35 g/1¼ oz
shallots, finely
sliced

1 tomato,
skinned, deseeded
and finely diced

salt and white
pepper

THE VINAIGRETTE
1 raw beetroot

salt and white
pepper

2 tbsp red wine
vinegar

½ shallot,
finely chopped

200 ml/7 fl oz
extra virgin
olive oil

Suggested wine:
Liquoroso 'Vigna
la miccia', De
Bartoli, Sicilia

This is a fantastic summer dish for June or
July when broad beans and peas are in season.
I always skin the peas becuase they look and
taste so much better like this. However,
if you are short of time or find this a
frustrating task you can leave them unskinned.
Steaming the foie gras - a very simple
procedure - will rid it of any fatty taste.
The sea salt and the beetroot vinaigrette
help to bring out its wonderful flavour.
I use duck foie gras, as goose is available
only for a limited season.

First prepare the vinaigrette. Peel the beetroot and grate it into a
shallow bowl, then turn it, with its juices, into a sieve over another
bowl or jug. Press down with a spoon to extract as much juice as you
can. Reserve the juice and keep the grated beetroot for a salad or
another use. Add the salt and pepper to the red wine vinegar and whisk
to dissolve the salt; you need to add the seasoning before you add the
oil, or the salt won't dissolve properly. Add the chopped shallot and
the beetroot juice, and whisk while pouring in the olive oil in a slow,
steady stream.
Blanch the broad beans and peas together in boiling water for 10
seconds. Drain and refresh in cold water. When they are cool, skin the
beans and the peas (but see above).
Fill a pan or steamer three-quarters full with the court-bouillon and
heat until simmering. Place the foie gras in the steamer over the top,
replace the lid and steam for 7-8 minutes until cooked. Heat the olive
oil in a pan and cook the shallots gently until soft and golden. Add the
broad beans and peas to heat through, then season to taste. Add the
diced tomato and toss to combine.
Place the bean, pea and tomato mixture in the centre of a large serving
plate or 4 individual plates, shaping into a round. Place the foie gras
slices on the top, season with sea salt and drizzle the vinaigrette all
around.

❷

Insalata di scampi e asparagi, pomodori secchi, vinaigrette di crostacei

SALAD OF LANGOUSTINES AND ASPARAGUS WITH SUNDRIED TOMATOES AND SHELLFISH VINAIGRETTE

20 medium
langoustines, or
tiger prawns

16 green
asparagus stalks

zest of 1 unwaxed
lemon

4 sundried
tomatoes, drained
if in oil,
deseeded

8 black olives

125 g/4¹/₂ oz
rocket

85 g/3 oz frisée
lettuce

1 tbsp olive oil

THE SHELLFISH
VINAIGRETTE
heads from the
langoustines or
tiger prawns

olive oil

3 tbsp soy sauce

2 tomatoes,
quartered

200 g/7 oz fresh
root ginger,
peeled and
chopped

ice cubes, to
cover

red wine vinegar

Suggested wine:
Sauvignon 'Piere'
Vie de Romans,
1997, Friuli
Venezia Giulia

This is a perfect starter for early summer.
The slightly bitter taste of the rocket
complements the sweetness of the langoustines.
I like to use ginger to sharpen the
vinaigrette - it's not as harsh as chilli,
and adds an interesting piquancy.

First, make the shellfish vinaigrette. Cut the heads off the langoustines or prawns, then slice each head in half and rinse under cold water to clean. Set aside. Shell the tails, then devein them by lifting out the intestinal tract with the point of a sharp knife. Heat 1 tbsp oil in a large casserole, add the langoustine or prawn heads and cook for another 5 minutes until browned. Add the soy sauce, tomatoes and ginger and enough ice cubes to cover all the ingredients. Heat gently and bring to the boil, then simmer for 10-15 minutes. Pass the mixture through a chinois or fine-meshed sieve lined with muslin, and heat again in a clean pan until reduced by half. Allow to cool, then measure the liquid in a measuring jug. For every 90 ml/3 fl oz liquid, whisk in 2 tbsp vinegar and 150 ml/¼ pint olive oil.

You don't need to add any extra salt as the soy sauce is already very salty.

The vinaigrette will keep in the fridge for 1 week.
Prepare a bowl of iced water. Peel the tough skin from the base of the asparagus spears, then blanch them in plenty of boiling salted water for 6-7 minutes until tender. Refresh in the iced water and drain. Blanch the lemon zest in boiling water 3 times, removing the zest each time the water returns to the boil and refreshing in iced water. Slice the zest, sundried tomatoes and olives very finely.
Arrange the rocket on one half of each serving plate. Place the frisée in the centre of the plate and arrange the asparagus over this, with the tips resting on the rocket.
Heat 1 tbsp oil in a pan and sauté the langoustines or prawns for 4 minutes, then arrange them on the plate. Garnish with the lemon zest, sundried tomatoes and olives and dress with the shellfish vinaigrette.

Insalata di fegato grasso e spinaci all 'aceto balsamico

SALAD OF FOIE GRAS AND BABY SPINACH WITH BALSAMIC VINEGAR

3 eggs

150 g/5¹/₂ oz baby spinach

4 fresh foie gras slices, about 125 g/4¹/₂ oz each

salt and white pepper

50 ml/2 fl oz balsamic vinegar

120 ml/4 fl oz olive oil

Suggested wine: Gewurztraminer 'Kolbenhof' Hoftatter, 1997, Trentino Alto Adige

This very simple dish makes a good starter for a dinner party. Make sure that the spinach is young and tender, but that the balsamic vinegar, by contrast, is well aged.

Hardboil the eggs for 8 minutes until firm. Remove from the pan, cool under cold running water, and then peel off the shells.
Wash the spinach, then drain well and pat completely dry with paper towels. Place the spinach leaves on one large serving plate or 4 individual ones, overlapping them starting from the edges and working towards the centre.
Heat a non-stick pan, add the foie gras slices, season them and briefly panfry them, turning once, for 2 minutes on each side.
Carefully grate the chopped eggs into a bowl.
Place the foie gras slices on top of the spinach. Skim the fat from the pan and, over a medium heat, deglaze the pan with the balsamic vinegar. Add the olive oil and whisk to combine, season to taste, then pour over the foie gras and spinach. Sprinkle the grated egg over the top.

Insalata di pernice e mele

SALAD OF PARTRIDGE AND APPLE

4 partridges,
prepared for the
oven, or 8 partridge
breasts, skin on

300 g/10¹/₂ oz
goose or duck fat,
melted

1¹/₄ tbsp olive oil

1 thyme sprig

2 garlic cloves,
crushed

salt and freshly
ground white pepper

2 eating apples,
such as Cox's

juice of 1 lemon

40 g/1¹/₂ oz sugar

4 slices back
bacon

85 g/3 oz green
beans

4 fresh foie gras
slices, about
125 g/4¹/₂ oz each

100 ml/3¹/₂ fl oz
partridge jus or
chicken jus
(see pages 17-18)

20 g/³/₄ oz butter

THE VINAIGRETTE
1 tbsp white wine
vinegar

salt and white
pepper

4 tbsp olive oil

Suggested wine:
Pinot nero 'San
Valentin' San
Michele Appiano,
1995, Trentino
Alto Adige

I love the combination of partridge and apple.
It's a great dish for mid-October or November,
when partridge is at its best. Be careful not
to colour the apple slices too much or they
will taste burnt. You can leave out the foie
gras and the partridge legs confit to make
a lighter dish, if you prefer.

Ask your butcher to joint the whole partridge, if using, and remove the
breast meat from the bone. Reserve the carcass if you are making the
partridge jus and keep the legs to make the confit. For the confit,
preheat the oven to 100°C/175°F/gas mark low. Place the partridge legs
in a small roasting pan, then cover with the melted goose or duck fat.
Cover with dampened, crumpled greaseproof paper to keep the legs
submerged in the fat. Put the pan over a medium heat on the hob and
bring the fat to the boil. Very carefully transfer the pan to the oven
and cook for 1 hour or until the meat is tender and comes easily away
from the bone.
Remove from the oven and leave the legs to cool in the fat. Strip the
meat from the bones and set aside. You can reuse the fat; pass it
through a sieve 2 or 3 times, then store in the fridge, covered, for up
to 2 months.
Heat the olive oil in a pan, add the thyme, garlic and partridge
breasts, season and sauté for 3-4 minutes on each side, until brown on
the outside and pink in the middle. Remove from the pan, cover and leave
to rest for 5-10 minutes.
Preheat the grill to medium high. Peel and core the apples and slice
thinly. Place on a grill pan lined with kitchen foil and sprinkle with
the lemon juice and sugar. Grill for 4-5 minutes, turning once, until
the sugar has melted and the apple slices are brown and caramelized.
Remove from the grill pan and set aside. Grill the bacon until crisp.
Make the vinaigrette. Pour the vinegar into a small bowl or cup, add a
good pinch of salt and pepper and whisk until the salt has dissolved.
Add the oil and whisk again.
Prepare a bowl of iced water. Cook the beans in plenty of salted boiling
water for 4-5 minutes, then refresh in the water and drain. Cut the
beans in half and combine with the partridge leg meat and vinaigrette.
Divide among 4 serving plates and top each with a piece of bacon.
Heat a non-stick pan and sauté the foie gras for 2 minutes on each side.
Place 1 slice on each plate with 2 partridge breasts. Arrange the apples
over the breasts. Heat the partridge jus, whisk in the butter and pour a
little over each serving.

❺

Insalata di alzavole e lenticchie

SALAD OF TEAL AND LENTILS

4 teal or duck,
prepared for the
oven or 8 teal
or duck breasts,
skin on

400 g/14 oz
Casteluccio or Puy
lentils

8 tbsp olive oil

1 onion, roughly
chopped

1 carrot, roughly
chopped

1 celery stalk,
roughly chopped

about 300 ml/½
pint vegetable
stock

1 bouquet garni
(see page 188)

salt and white
pepper

2 slices back bacon

4 garlic cloves,
crushed

2 thyme sprigs

2 rosemary sprigs

50 g/1¾ oz butter

12 quail's eggs

100 g/3½ oz
frisée lettuce

1 tbsp vinaigrette
(see page 189)

75 ml/2½ fl oz
teal, duck or
chicken jus (see
pages 17-18)

Suggested wine:
Soave Classico 'Du
Lot' Inama, 1996,
Veneto

Teal is the most delicate-tasting bird in
the duck family, and goes very well with
the earthy flavour of lentils. If you can't
find teal, use duck instead.

Ask your butcher to joint the whole teal, if using, and remove the
breast meat from the bone. Reserve the carcass if you are making the jus
and keep the legs for another dish.
Soak the lentils in a large pan of cold water overnight, then drain and
rinse. Heat 2 tbsp olive oil in a casserole, add the onion, carrot and
celery and sauté for 3-4 minutes. Add the lentils and sauté for another
5 minutes. Heat the vegetable stock in a separate pan, then pour in
enough stock to cover and add the bouquet garni. Bring to the boil and
simmer for 20 minutes or until the lentils are tender.
Preheat the grill to medium high, then cook the bacon until crispy. When
cool, slice each piece of bacon in half.
When the lentils are ready, strain them, reserving the cooking water but
discarding the onion, carrot and celery and bouquet garni. Blend half of
the lentils to a purée with a little of the cooking water. Mix with the
whole lentils and season to taste.
Place 5 tbsp olive oil in a casserole with the garlic cloves, thyme and
rosemary and heat very gently for 10 minutes to infuse the garlic with
the flavours. Remove from the heat and leave to stand for 5 minutes.
Strain into the pan containing the lentils, stirring to combine.
Heat 1 tbsp olive oil in a pan. Add the teal breasts, season and sauté
for 2-3 minutes on each side until brown on the outside and pink in the
middle. Remove from the pan, cover and leave to rest for 5 minutes.
Slice each breast diagonally into 3 pieces.
Melt 35 g/1¼ oz butter in a frying pan and fry the quail's eggs. Slide
on to a plate lined with kitchen paper.
Divide the lentils among 4 warmed soup plates. Toss the frisée with the
vinaigrette and place on top of the lentils. Arrange the fried quail's
eggs and sliced teal breast around the frisée and garnish with the
crispy bacon. Reheat the jus and whisk in the remaining butter. Season
to taste and spoon over the teal and lentils.

❻

Insalata di patate, carciofi e formaggio di capra

POTATO SALAD WITH TOMATOES, ARTICHOKES AND GOAT'S CHEESE

10 new potatoes

2 plum tomatoes

6 baby artichokes

lemon juice

1 tbsp olive oil

1 garlic clove, chopped

1 thyme sprig

100 ml/3¹/₂ fl oz dry white wine

100 ml/3¹/₂ fl oz vegetable stock (see page 17)

150 g/5¹/₂ oz mixed leaves, radicchio, rucola, baby spinach and frisée

125 g/4¹/₂ oz goat's cheese

THE VINAIGRETTE
20 g/¹/₂ oz salt

100 ml/3¹/₂ fl oz red wine vinegar

300 ml/10 fl oz extra virgin olive oil

Suggested wine: Chardonnay Isole Colene, 1997, Toscana

Every good meal should start with a salad. This simple, summery dish combines distinctly different textures and flavours and can be adapted to include whatever vegetables you have to hand.

Cook the new potatoes in their skins in boiling salted water until tender. Drain and refresh in cold water. Peel them when they are cool enough to handle. Blanch the tomatoes for a few seconds and refresh under cold water. Skin them, then cut into quarters and remove the seeds.
Peel off the tough outer leaves of the artichokes until you reach the tender heart, then cut off the top third and scoop out the choke. Slice off a small amount of the green stalk at the bottom.

When preparing artichokes, always place them in a bowl of acidulated water (water with lemon juice) until you are ready to cook them, otherwise the inner leaves and heart may go brown once they come into contact with the air.

Heat the olive oil in a pan, then add the garlic and thyme. After 30 seconds add the artichokes and wine, then cover the pan with a lid. When the wine has evaporated, add the vegetable stock, cover and cook for another 5-7 minutes. Once the stock has evaporated the artichokes should be cooked and tender.
Make the vinaigrette. Mix the salt with the vinegar, then add the oil gradually, whisking between each addition.
Toss the salad leaves with some of the vinaigrette, then distribute the leaves among 4 plates or 1 large serving dish. Toss the potatoes, artichokes and tomatoes with the remaining vinaigrette and place them over the salad leaves. Slice the goat's cheese and divide among the plates.

❼

Crema fredda di pomodoro, scampi al vapore, cetriolo e caviale

---

COLD TOMATO SOUP WITH STEAMED LANGOUSTINES, CUCUMBER AND CAVIARE

100 g/3½ oz
peeled cucumber,
roughly chopped,
plus ¼ medium
cucumber

500 g/1 lb 2 oz
ripe tomatoes,
roughly chopped

100 g/3½ oz red
pepper, deseeded
and roughly
chopped

10 g/¼ oz onion

2 garlic cloves,
finely chopped

pinch of salt

20 medium
langoustines, or
tiger prawns,
shelled and
deveined

500 ml/18 fl oz
court-bouillon
(see page 16)

200 ml/7 fl oz
whipping cream

juice of 1 lemon

50 g/1¾ oz
caviare

chervil, to
garnish

Suggested wine:
Vermentino di
Gallura
Capicchiera,
1998, Sardegna

This is a very refreshing summery dish – the chilled tomato soup is similar to a Spanish gazpacho. The cool cucumber flavour contrasts beautifully with the sweet flesh of the langoustines. I like to use Italian tomatoes from Pachino – make sure the ones you use are very ripe, preferably on the vine.

Place the chopped cucumber in a food processor with the tomatoes, pepper, onion, garlic and salt, and pulse to a purée. Pass the purée through a chinois or fine-meshed sieve. Divide among 4 soup plates. Cut the ¼ cucumber in half lengthways, then slice the flesh with a mandoline or very sharp knife to make 20 thin, almost transparent, rectangular slices. Wrap the slices round the langoustines or prawns. Heat the court-bouillon in a pan and place the wrapped langoustines in a steamer that fits over the top of the pan. Steam for 5-6 minutes. Remove the langoustines and arrange 5 on top of each serving of soup.
In a shallow non-metallic bowl lightly whip the cream, then gently fold the lemon juice into the cream with a wooden spoon. Using a teaspoon, place a little cream on top of each langoustine, then top with some caviare. Garnish with chervil.

8

Fiori di zucchina fritti, farciti al pomodoro e mozzarella, salsa agrodolce

DEEP-FRIED COURGETTE FLOWERS STUFFED WITH TOMATO AND MOZZARELLA, WITH A SWEET-AND-SOUR SAUCE

300 g/12 oz strong white flour

1 pinch bicarbonate of soda

150 ml/5 fl oz iced water

2 tbsp sweet-and-sour sauce (see page 21)

8 large courgette flowers with courgettes attached

1 x 200 g/8 oz ball buffalo mozzarella, cubed

50 g/1³/₄ oz tomato concassée (1 tomato)

2 anchovies, finely chopped

2 basil leaves, finely chopped

salt and white pepper

2 tbsp olive oil

500 ml/18 fl oz vegetable oil

Suggested wine: Tocai, Borgo San Daniele Friuli Venezia Giulia

This is a classic Roman recipe. Make sure you drain the mozzarella well before using - any excess water will stop the batter round the courgette flowers from crisping up properly when you fry them.

First, prepare the batter. In a bowl mix the flour with the bicarbonate of soda. Add the iced water and whisk until a smooth paste forms. Set aside in the fridge to rest for about 2 hours. While the batter is resting, prepare the sweet-and-sour sauce.

Remove the flowers from the courgettes and scoop out their fleshy insides. Slice the courgettes into thin rounds and set aside. Place the cubed mozzarella in a mixing bowl. Add half of the tomato concassée, and the anchovies and basil, and season. Gently open each of the courgette flowers and fill with equal portions of the mozzarella mixture.

In a shallow pan warm the sweet-and-sour sauce and add the rest of the tomato. Leave over a low heat to warm gradually while you sauté the courgettes.

Heat the olive oil in a pan and sauté the courgettes until golden, then divide among 4 warmed serving plates.

Heat the vegetable oil in a deep frying pan to a temperature of about 170°C/325°F/gas mark 3. With a pair of chopsticks dip each courgette flower in the batter, making sure it is evenly coated, then fry in the oil until lightly golden - about 2 minutes. Remove from the oil with a slotted spoon and drain, then pat dry on paper towels. Cut the flowers carefully in half and place on top of the bed of courgettes. Spoon the warmed sauce around the plates.

❾

Tonno marinato all 'aceto balsamico e salsa di soya

MARINATED TUNA IN BALSAMIC VINEGAR AND SOY SAUCE

400 g/14 oz tuna
loin, cut into
1 cm x 1 cm/^{1}/$_2$ in
x ^{1}/$_2$ in cubes

85 g/3 oz
courgette skin
(the skin from 2
medium
courgettes)

85 g/3 oz daikon
radish

85 g/3 oz carrots

chervil, to
garnish

THE MARINADE
2 tbsp sweet-
and-sour sauce
(see page 21)

piece of fresh
root ginger,
about 150 g/
5^1/$_2$ oz

75 ml/2^1/$_2$ fl oz
balsamic vinegar

3 tbsp soy sauce

^{3}/$_4$ tbsp salt

450 ml/16 fl oz
olive oil

Suggested wine:
Chardonnay
Selezioni 'Borgo
del Tiglio',
1996, Friuli
Venezia Giulia

The oriental flavours in this recipe are
complemented by the Italian flavours of
balsamic vinegar and olive oil, which give
the tuna a sensational taste. It's essential
that the tuna you use is very fresh. You can
buy daikon radish from oriental grocers and
Asian stores.

To make the marinade, have ready the sweet-and-sour sauce. Peel the
ginger and grate it, then press it in a fine-meshed sieve or chinois
with the back of a spoon to yield about 2 tbsp juice. In a bowl, mix the
juice with all the other marinade ingredients except the olive oil. Add
the oil last, whisking it as you pour it in gradually.
Place the cubed tuna in a shallow dish and pour over the marinade. Leave
for 5-10 minutes in the fridge - the marinade will 'cook' the tuna.
Cut the courgette skin, daikon and carrots into fine julienne strips.

As you prepare them, put the vegetable strips into a bowl of iced water - this
helps to keep them crisp.

Drain the vegetable strips and distribute them among four serving
plates, then place the tuna on top, together with a little marinade as a
dressing. Garnish with chervil.

Vitello tonnato

FILLET OF VEAL IN TUNA AND MAYONNAISE SAUCE

600 g/1 lb 5 oz
veal fillet

salt and white
pepper

85 g/3 oz mixed
salad leaves

THE SAUCE
200 g/7 oz tuna
fish in oil,
drained

85 g/3 oz
mayonnaise (about
5 tbsp)

2 anchovies,
chopped

20 g/$^{3}/_{4}$ oz
capers, rinsed
and chopped, plus
extra to garnish

100 ml/3$^{1}/_{2}$ fl oz
single cream

THE VINAIGRETTE
50 ml/2 fl oz red
wine vinegar

150 ml/5 fl oz
olive oil

salt and black
pepper

Suggested wine:
Chardonnay
Jearman, 1997,
Friuli Venezia
Giulia

This is a classic Piemontese recipe.
My version is inspired by Gualtiero Marchesi,
whom I worked for in Milan, and who decided
to part with tradition by placing the meat
on top of the sauce instead of the other way
round. This method of cooking the veal helps
to keep it meltingly tender. Try to use the
best quality canned tuna you can find.

Trim the fat from the veal fillet and season the meat with salt and
pepper. Wrap it tightly in clingfilm so that no meat is exposed. Heat a
pan of water to 60°C/150°F - the water should not be boiling - and place
the veal in the water. Cook for 1½ hours, keeping the heat very low and
the water at 60°C/150°F - use a heat diffuser if necessary. Remove the
veal from the water and check the temperature at the centre of the meat
using a meat thermometer - it should be at 60°C/150°F. Leave to cool in
the clingfilm, then refrigerate for 2 hours. Cut into fine slices.
To make the sauce, put the tuna, mayonnaise, anchovies and capers in the
bowl of a food processor and blend to a purée. Pass the sauce through a
sieve into a bowl and add the cream, stirring to combine.
Make the vinaigrette. Mix the oil with the vinegar, then add the oil
gradually. Toss with the salad leaves.
Pour a little sauce on to each serving plate, spreading it out carefully
with the back of a spoon. Place the veal slices over the sauce and top
with a few salad leaves. Garnish with capers, dotting them around the
sauce.

⬤⬤

Sfogliatina di scampi, asparagi e tartufo

FEUILLETE OF LANGOUSTINES, ASPARAGUS AND TRUFFLE

500 g/1 lb 2 oz
puff pastry (see
page 22)

1 egg yolk,
beaten

250 ml/9 fl oz
asparagus sauce
(see page 19)

12 asparagus
stalks

1 tbsp olive oil

12 large
langoustines, or
tiger prawns,
shelled and
deveined

35 g/1¼ oz black
truffle, finely
chopped
(optional)

Suggested wine:
Verdicchio dei
'Castelli di
Jesi' Santarelli
1997

This beautifully simple starter makes an
elegant dish for a dinner party. Make sure
you cook the pastry until it is really golden
and flaky.

Preheat the oven to 220°C/425°F/gas mark 7.
Roll out the puff pastry very thinly (to about 5 mm/¼in) on a lightly
floured worksurface and cut it into 4 squares 10 x 10 cm/4 x 4 in. Brush
each square with beaten egg yolk and lift on to the baking sheet. Cook
in the oven for 20-25 minutes until golden and puffed up.
Prepare the asparagus sauce and set aside; do not add the olive oil
until you are ready to serve.
Prepare a bowl of iced water. Trim the woody end from the asparagus
stalks then cook the stalks in plenty of boiling salted water for 5
minutes until tender. Refresh in the iced water, then drain. Trim the
asparagus tips to about 5 cm/2 in then set them aside. Chop the
remaining asparagus into small even pieces.
Carefully cut a square lid out of the top of each puff-pastry case,
leaving the base intact, to make a hollow for the langoustines and
asparagus. Scoop out some of the inside and reserve the pastry lids.
Heat the olive oil in a pan and sauté the langoustines or tiger prawns
for about 4 minutes. Remove from the oil and set aside.
Over a gentle heat whisk the olive oil into the asparagus sauce and add
the pieces of asparagus and the chopped truffle to finish.
Spoon a little sauce over each serving plate and place one puff pastry
case on top. Fill each pastry case with 3 langoustines or prawns and 3
asparagus tips, and rest the pastry lid over the top at an angle.

⑫

Uova bazzotte al tartufo nero e scampi saltati

BOILED SCRAMBLED EGGS WITH BLACK TRUFFLE AND LANGOUSTINES

1 tbsp olive oil

16 large langoustines or tiger prawns, shelled and deveined

12 eggs

40 g/1½ oz black truffle, finely chopped, plus 15 g/½ oz black truffle, finely sliced

salt and white pepper

chervil, to garnish

Suggested wine: Bianco Miani, 1996, Friuli Venezia Giulia

My mother always used to make scrambled eggs for me in this way before I went to school in the morning; cooking them like this sets the white, while keeping the yolk runny. I've added the truffle and the langoustines to make a more luxurious version, but you could substitute wild mushrooms sautéed in oil and garlic, or leave the eggs plain and simple. Try to use the freshest eggs you can - organic if possible.

In a sauté pan heat the oil and sauté the langoustines or prawns for 4 minutes.
Cook the eggs in boiling water for 3 minutes. Remove them immediately from the water, then, using a cloth to protect your hands, slice in half with a knife. Hold the eggs over a pan and, using a teaspoon, scoop the whites and yolks into the pan.
Add the chopped truffle to the eggs, then season. Over a very gentle heat whisk the eggs for 1 minute, being careful not to overcook the yolks. Place the eggs in soup bowls and place 4 sautéed langoustines or prawns over each serving. Top with slices of truffle and garnish with chervil.

⓭

Soufflé di sogliole con salsa di piselli e pomodori confit

SOLE SOUFFLE WITH FRESH PEA SAUCE AND TOMATO CONFIT

200 ml/7 fl oz
pea sauce (see
page 19)

3 tomatoes confit
(see page 188),
quartered

250 g/9 oz Dover
sole fillets,
skinned, for the
purée, plus 8
Dover sole
fillets, skinned,
to garnish

1 egg, plus 1 egg
white

salt and white
pepper

250 ml/9 fl oz
whipping cream

50 g/1³/₄ oz
butter

100 g/3¹/₂ oz
black truffle,
finely sliced

500 ml/18 fl oz
court-bouillon
(see page 16)

olive oil, to
serve

Suggested wine:
Sauvignon 'Ronco
delle mele'
Venica, 1997,
Friuli Venezia
Giulia

Don't be afraid of making soufflé - this recipe is really quite straightforward. Sole and peas both have delicate, fresh flavours that harmonize perfectly in this dish. You can substitute shellfish for sole, if you prefer - just increase the volume of shellfish meat to 375 g/13 oz.

Prepare the pea sauce, but do not whisk in the olive oil until you are ready to serve. Make the tomatoes confit.
Preheat the oven to 190°C/375°F/gas mark 5. Put the 250 g/9 oz of sole fillets in a food processor with the egg, egg white and a pinch of salt. Process to a fine purée. At this stage you can pass the purée through a chinois or fine-meshed sieve if you want a really fine texture. Whip the cream until just starting to thicken, then carefully stir it into the sole purée, and season.

To help the soufflé rise, stir in the cream very gradually, a third at a time, and allow the mixture to rest for 10-20 minutes between each addition.

Put the kettle on to boil. Grease 4 individual ceramic soufflé dishes, about 5-6 cm/2-2½ in in diameter, with the butter and spread the truffle slices over the base. Carefully spoon the soufflé mix into each dish then tap the dishes sharply on the worksurface to get rid of any bubbles. Put the soufflés in a deep baking tray and place on the oven shelf. Pour in hot (not boiling) water to come halfway up the sides of the dishes. Cook for 16-18 minutes, until risen evenly - check to see if the soufflés are done by inserting a toothpick into the centre. If it emerges clean, the soufflés are ready.
About 5 minutes before the soufflés are ready, poach the remaining sole fillets in the court-bouillon for 2 minutes, until tender. Lift out with a slotted spoon and set aside.
Gently heat the pea sauce and whisk in the olive oil to finish.
Loosen around the edge of each soufflé with a knife, then carefully turn them out on to a warmed serving plate. Spoon the sauce around the soufflé and garnish with the sole and the tomatoes confit, giving each person 4 pieces of sole and 3 tomato quarters. For a finishing touch, drizzle a little extra olive oil over before serving.

❶④

Sella di coniglio impanata al rosmarino, salsa ai carciofi

BREADED SADDLE OF RABBIT WITH ROSEMARY AND ARTICHOKE SAUCE

2 saddles of rabbit, including the best end and rib cage

4 tbsp rabbit jus or chicken jus (see pages 17-18)

125 ml/4 fl oz artichoke sauce (see page 19)

2 eggs

1 rosemary sprig, finely chopped

150 g/5$\frac{1}{2}$ oz fresh breadcrumbs

125 g/4$\frac{1}{2}$ oz butter

12 baby artichokes

lemon juice

2 tbsp olive oil

2 garlic cloves, crushed

2 thyme sprigs

3 tbsp dry white wine

300 ml/$\frac{1}{2}$ pint vegetable stock (see page 17)

50 g/1$\frac{3}{4}$ oz tomato concassée (1 tomato)

125 g/4$\frac{1}{2}$ oz frisée lettuce

chervil, to garnish

1 tbsp vinaigrette (see page 189)

Suggested wine: Chardonnay 'Castel de Ringberg' Elena Watch 1997 Trentino Alto Adige

Rabbit has a delicate flavour that goes very well with artichokes. Rosemary is used a great deal in Italian cooking, especially for roasting meat. Don't season the rabbit before you cook it - any salt would draw the juices out of the meat and make the bread crust go soggy. Instead use salted butter to add seasoning.

Ask your butcher to bone the rabbit saddles. Reserve the bones and rib cage if you are making the rabbit jus.
Prepare the artichoke sauce.
Whisk the eggs in a bowl and combine the rosemary with the breadcrumbs in another bowl. Dip the rabbit first in the beaten egg, then in the breadcrumbs, and repeat 2 or 3 times until it is well coated. Melt 100 g/3½ oz of the butter in a pan and cook the rabbit for about 3 minutes on each side until the breadcrumbs have formed a golden crust (you may need to do this in 2 batches). Peel off the tough outer leaves of the artichokes until you reach the tender heart, then cut off the top third and scoop out the choke using a teaspoon. Slice off a small amount of the green stalk at the bottom. Place the artichokes in a bowl of acidulated water (water with lemon juice) until you are ready to cook them (see page 36).
Heat 1 tbsp olive oil in a large pan, then add the garlic and thyme. After 30 seconds add the artichokes and wine, then cover the pan with a lid. When the wine has evaporated, add the vegetable stock, cover and cook for another 10 minutes until tender. Remove the artichokes from the liquid and fill each one with the tomato concassée. Gently heat the artichoke sauce and whisk in 1 tbsp olive oil. In a separate pan heat the rabbit jus or stock and whisk in the remaining butter.
Make the vinaigrette and toss with the frisée.
Arrange the frisée in the centre of 4 warmed serving plates. Place 3 artichokes on top of each serving, and spoon the sauce and the jus around the frisée. Slice the rabbit into pieces and place it on top of the sauce. Garnish with chervil.

Primi piatti

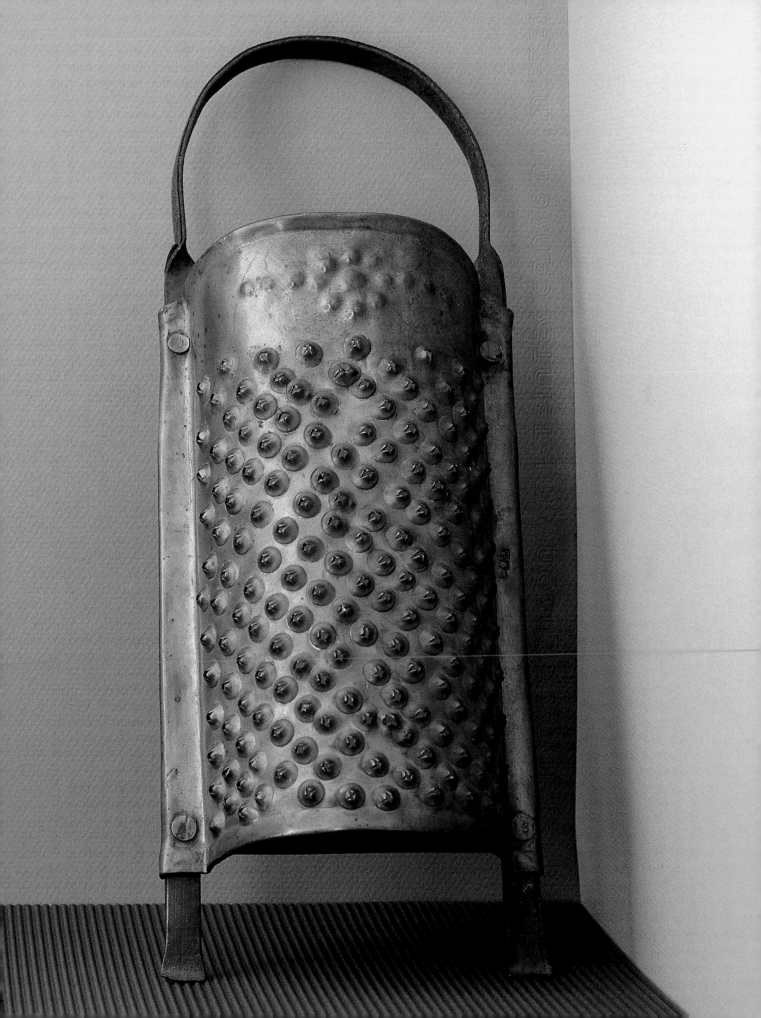

masterclass 2: pasta

BASIC PASTA DOUGH
Makes 400 g/14 oz

300 g/10¹/₂ oz
plain flour
(type 00)

pinch of salt

3 eggs

2 tsp olive oil

SPINACH PASTA DOUGH
Makes 600 g/1 lb
5 oz

100 g/3¹/₂ oz
spinach

500 g/1 lb 2oz
plain flour

pinch of salt

3-4 eggs

2 tbsp olive oil

SQUID INK PASTA DOUGH
Makes 400 g/14 oz

3 eggs

1 tbsp squid ink

300 g/10¹/₂ oz
flour

pinch of salt

1 tbsp olive oil

Homemade pasta is simple and satisfying to make. You'll need a wooden worksurface, a simple cranked machine with thinning rollers, a fork, tea towels, clingfilm and pastry cutters.

Making the dough

1 Sieve the flour and salt on to a wooden surface and shape into a rough mound. Make a well in the centre, and crack the eggs into the well. Drizzle the oil around the flour.

2 Using a fork, beat the eggs lightly, then gradually draw in the flour until the mixture is no longer runny. Using your hands, draw in enough flour to make a smooth dough. It should be neither too dry nor too moist. Wrap tightly in clingfilm and leave to rest for 3-4 hours in the fridge, or overnight.

Kneading the dough

1 Scrape the worksurface and wash and dry your hands. Using the heel of your palms, press the dough away from you. Fold in half, turn it by 180°, then repeat. Keep kneading and turning in the same direction for 4-5 minutes until the dough is smooth and elastic. If it feels dry, dampen your hands and knead again. If wet, add a little more flour.

2 Shape the dough into a ball.

Thinning the dough

1 Divide the dough into 8 equal pieces weighing about 50 g/1¾oz. Wrap all but 1 ball of dough tightly in cling film and set aside.

2 Set the pasta machine to its largest opening. Flatten the dough until it is nearly as wide as the rollers then pass it through the machine.

3 Feed the dough through once more and repeat until smooth.

4 Reduce the size of the opening by 1 notch and feed the dough through again. Continue reducing by 1 notch until you reach the desired thickness. Dust lightly with flour if the dough gets too sticky. Lay the pasta sheet flat on a lightly floured worksurface and cover with a clean kitchen towel as you roll out the other balls.

SPINACH PASTA DOUGH

1 Blanch the spinach leaves in plenty of salted boiling water. Refresh in cold water and drain thoroughly, squeezing out as much water as possible. Blend to a purée in a processor.

2 Proceed as for the basic dough, adding the purée before drawing in the flour. If the mixture seems too dry, add an extra egg.

SQUID INK PASTA DOUGH
Whisk the eggs with the squid ink, then proceed as for the basic dough.

Pappardelle
❶ Using a pastry wheel, cut the pasta sheet into pieces 30 cm/12 in long and then into strips 2 cm/¾ in wide.

❷ Leave to dry for 5 minutes. Pick up the pappardelle in batches and twirl into nests on a tray dusted with semolina flour.

Tagliolini and tagliatelle
❶ Place the pasta sheet with the long edges towards you and mark the centre point.

❷ Roll each of the short edges towards the centre point to make 2 parallel tubes.

❸ Using a sharp knife, cut across the width of the tubes at 1 cm/½ in intervals for tagliolini or ½ cm/¼ in for tagliatelle.

❹ Leave to dry for 5 minutes. Insert the tip of a knife into the centre of the tubes and lift up, shaking out the pasta into strips. Twirl into nests on a tray dusted with semolina flour.

Stracci
Using a pastry wheel, cut the pasta into 6 cm/2¼ in squares. Cut each square in half to make triangles.

Garganelli
I use a special stick and a ridged mat for making garganelli (which resemble penne).

❶ Using a pastry wheel, cut the pasta sheet into small 4 cm/1½ in squares.

❷ Place each square on the mat and smooth it over the ridges. Wrap one corner of the square round the middle of the stick. Turn the stick to roll the pasta into a tube, then gently slide the tube off.

Ravioli
Stuffed pasta should be filled and cut immediately, but can be made up to 1 day in advance; allow it to dry out thoroughly before covering with clingfilm and refrigerating. Alternatively, freeze for up to 1 month and cook from frozen for 1 minute longer.

❶ Using a piping bag or teaspoon, spoon the filling across one half of the pasta sheet in even rows, spacing them apart according to the size you wish to make. Work quickly so the dough does not dry out. If the pasta becomes dry, dampen with water or brush with eggwash.

❷ Carefully lower the other half of the sheet to cover the first half. Press to remove air.

❸ Use a pastry wheel to cut into individual squares between the fillings. Press the edges well to seal the filling.

Tortelloni and tortellini
❶ Using a pastry wheel, cut the pasta sheet into squares - 6 cm/2¼ in for tortelloni or 4 cm/1½ in for tortellini.

❷ Pipe the filling or place with a teaspoon in the middle of each square.

❸ Fold the pasta over the filling to make a triangle, then press well to seal the edges. Fold the filled triangle round your index finger and press the tips together.

Ravioli di cappesante, salsa basilico

SCALLOP RAVIOLI WITH BASIL SAUCE

150-200 g/5½-
7 oz basil leaves

2 tbsp olive oil,
plus extra for
grilling scallops

salt and white
pepper

THE RAVIOLI
18 small or
medium scallops,
cleaned and roes
removed

2 tbsp soy sauce

150 g/5½ oz
fresh pasta dough
(see page 56)

100g/3½ oz
tomatoes concassées
(2 tomatoes)

2 basil leaves,
finely chopped

Suggested wine:
Sauvignon Poggio
alle Gazze Tenuta
Ornellaia, 1998,
Toscana

For best results try to make the ravioli at the last minute. If you cook them from frozen the scallops will be overdone by the time the pasta is cooked; if you refrigerate them the scallops will make the pasta go soggy and break up during cooking.

Place 12 scallops in a shallow bowl, spoon over the soy sauce and leave to marinate in the fridge for 5-10 minutes. Slice the remaining 6 scallops in half horizontally and set aside. Prepare the pasta dough and divide into 6 even pieces. Pass the dough through the pasta machine, finishing at the lowest setting, until you have 6 very thin, almost transparent sheets. Transfer to a lightly floured surface. Using a 14 cm/5½ in round pasta cutter, cut the pasta into 12 circles. Place 1 scallop in the middle of each pasta circle and top it with a little of the tomato concassée and chopped basil. Bring the edges of the circle up over the scallop and pinch together in the middle to make a ridge. Prepare a bowl of iced water. Blanch the basil leaves in boiling salted water, then refresh in the iced water and drain. Transfer to a blender and pulse to a purée, adding the olive oil in a steady stream. Season to taste. Pass the basil sauce through a chinois or fine-meshed sieve into a clean pan and heat gently.

Cook the ravioli in plenty of salted boiling water for 3-4 minutes, then drain. While the pasta is cooking heat a ridged grill pan and sprinkle the scallop halves with salt and olive oil. Grill the scallops in the pan for 1 minute on each side.

Spoon the sauce around 4 warmed serving plates, then place 3 ravioli and 3 scallop halves per person over the top.

Ravioli di anatra, verze e fegato grasso

DUCK RAVIOLI WITH SAVOY CABBAGE AND FOIE GRAS

100 ml/3½ fl oz
Torcolato wine, or
good quality sweet
white wine

150 ml/¼ pint
duck jus or chicken
jus (see pages 17-
18)

12 fresh foie gras
pieces, about
25 g/1 oz each
(optional)

100 g/3½ oz savoy
cabbage

40 g/1½ oz butter

THE RAVIOLI
300 g/10½ oz duck
breast, skinned
and roughly chopped

100 ml/3½ fl oz
madeira

1 shallot, finely
chopped

1 tbsp olive oil

20 g/¾ oz
courgette skin and
carrot brunoise
(equal quantities
of each, very
finely diced)

85 ml/3 fl oz
whipping cream

salt and white
pepper

150 g/5½ oz fresh
pasta dough (see
page 56)

semolina flour

Suggested wine:
Malvasia Istriana
Selezione Borgo del
Tiglio, 1996,
Friuli Venezia
Giulia

This lovely winter dish was inspired by a conversation I had with Emanuele Lionello, a friend of mine at the Hotel Formentor in Mallorca. The sweetness of the Torcolato really brings out the best in the duck and foie gras. You can leave out the foie gras if you prefer something a little lighter.

First, make the filling for the ravioli. Put the chopped duck breast in a food processor or blender and pulse to a purée. Put the madeira and shallot in a pan and heat until reduced by half. Strain the liquid, then stir it into the duck purée. Leave to cool slightly then place in the fridge for about 30 minutes.

Heat the olive oil in a pan, add the courgette skin and carrot brunoise and sauté for 2-3 minutes. Add to the duck purée mixture and stir to combine. Add the cream gradually, stirring until smooth. Season to taste.

Make sure the duck purée is nice and cold before you add the cream, otherwise it may split.

Make the pasta dough and divide into 4 equal pieces. Pass it through the pasta machine, finishing at the lowest setting, until you have 4 very thin, almost transparent sheets (see page 56). Transfer to a lightly floured surface. Using a teaspoon, place small mounds of the filling along one half of the pasta sheet, spacing them evenly and leaving a gap of 4 cm/1½ in between each mound, and 2 cm/1 in at each edge. Bring the other half of the pasta sheet over the first half and press carefully around the filling to remove any air. Cut the ravioli into circles using a 4 cm/1½ in round pastry cutter.

To make the sauce, heat the wine in a pan until reduced by one-third, then add the duck jus and reduce again by half.

Cook the duck ravioli in plenty of boiling salted water for 6-8 minutes until tender. Heat a non-stick pan and fry the foie gras, without any oil, for 2 minutes until brown on both sides.

Trim the cabbage, removing and discarding any tough outer leaves. Cut the leaves into triangles, then blanch in boiling salted water for 3 minutes. Drain the cabbage and divide the leaves among 4 serving plates. Drain the ravioli and place on top of the cabbage. Warm the sauce and whisk in the butter to finish. Spoon over the ravioli and top with the pieces of foie gras.

❸

Ravioli di coniglio con gamberi e fiori di zucchina

RABBIT RAVIOLI WITH CRAYFISH AND COURGETTE FLOWERS

2 tbsp olive oil

12 large crayfish or langoustines, shelled and deveined

150 ml/1¼ pint shellfish stock (see page 16)

8-10 courgette flowers, cleaned and torn into strips

THE RAVIOLI
1 tbsp olive oil

10 g/¼ oz courgette skin and carrot brunoise (equal amounts of each, very finely diced)

75 ml/2½ fl oz white wine

1 shallot, finely chopped

300 g/10½ oz rabbit meat, trimmed of fat and roughly chopped

chervil sprig, finely chopped

tarragon sprig, finely chopped

75 ml/2½ fl oz whipping cream

salt

200 g/7 oz fresh pasta dough (see page 56)

Suggested wine: Chardonnay Bussiador, 1996, (A. Coterno) Piemonte

I have made round ravioli in this recipe, but the shape of ravioli is really up to you: you can make them square, triangular or round. If you can't get hold of crayfish, use langoustines or tiger prawns instead.

For the ravioli, heat the olive oil in a pan and sauté the courgette skin and carrot brunoise for 3 minutes. Simmer the white wine and shallot in a separate pan until the liquid has reduced by half. Pulse the rabbit meat to a purée in a food processor or blender. For a really fine texture, pass the purée through a chinois or fine-meshed sieve. Transfer the purée to a bowl and add the reduced wine and shallot, the chervil and tarragon and the sautéed carrot and courgette mixture. Leave to cool, then refrigerate for a few minutes, then add the cream, stirring to combine. Season to taste with salt.
Make the pasta dough, then divide into 4 equal pieces. Pass the dough through the pasta machine finishing at the lowest setting, until you have 4 very thin, almost transparent sheets (see page 56). Transfer to a lightly floured surface. Make the stuffed pasta as for the duck ravioli (see page 60), spacing the filling 6 cm/2¼ in apart and leaving 3 cm/ 1 in at each edge. Cut out circles with a 6 cm/2¼ in round pastry cutter.
Heat 1 tbsp olive oil in a pan and sauté the crayfish for 4 minutes. Cook the ravioli in plenty of boiling salted water for 3-4 minutes, then drain. Pour the shellfish stock into a pan and heat until reduced by half. Whisk in 1 tbsp olive oil, then add the ravioli and courgette flowers.
Divide the ravioli and sauce among 4 warmed serving plates and top with 3 crayfish per person.

4

Ravioli di melanzane e taleggio, burro fuso e pinoli

AUBERGINE AND TALEGGIO RAVIOLI WITH MELTED BUTTER AND PINE NUTS

1 tbsp olive oil

100g/3¹/₂ oz
tomatoes concassées
(2 tomatoes)

2 basil leaves,
finely sliced
into julienne
strips

100 g/3¹/₂ oz
butter

40 g/1¹/₂ oz pine
nuts

THE RAVIOLI
2¹/₂ tbsp olive
oil

2 aubergines,
peeled and cut
into 1 x 1 cm/¹/₂
x ¹/₂ in cubes

salt and freshly
ground white
pepper

250 g/9 oz
taleggio cheese,
cut into 1 x 1
cm/¹/₂ x ¹/₂ in
cubes

4 basil leaves,
finely sliced
into julienne
strips

100 g/3¹/₂ oz
Parmesan cheese,
grated

200 g/7 oz fresh
pasta dough (see
page 56)

Suggested wine:
Vintage Tunina
Jermann, 1997,
Veneto

This is an excellent vegetarian pasta dish.
As the ravioli cook, the taleggio - a fresh-tasting soft cheese - melts around the
aubergine to make a delicious filling.
The toasted pine nuts add a contrasting
bite and a smoky, nutty flavour.

First make the filling for the ravioli. Heat the olive oil in a pan and
add the aubergine and seasoning. Cook for 10 minutes until tender.
Remove from the heat and leave to cool in the pan. Add the taleggio to
the aubergine, together with the basil and 85 g/3 oz of the grated
Parmesan and stir to combine.
Make the pasta dough and divide into 4 equal pieces. Pass it through the
pasta machine, finishing at the lowest setting, until you have 4 very
thin, almost transparent sheets (see page 56). Transfer to a lightly
floured surface. Make the stuffed pasta as for the duck ravioli (see
page 60), spacing the filling 5 cm/2 in apart, and 2¹/₂ cm/1 in from each
edge, and cutting out 5 x 5 cm/2 x 2 in squares. Use a fork to score the
edges lightly.
Cook the ravioli in plenty of boiling salted water for 5 minutes.
Meanwhile heat the olive oil in a pan, add the tomato concassée and
basil and sauté for 1 minute.
Melt the butter in a pan, drain the ravioli and toss with the butter.
Place 5 ravioli on each of 4 warmed serving plates, spoon the tomato and
basil mixture in the centre and scatter over the pine nuts and remaining
Parmesan.

❺

Tortelloni di fagiano con salsa di cavolfiori e tartufo nero

PHEASANT TORTELLONI WITH CAULIFLOWER SAUCE AND BLACK TRUFFLE

250 ml/9 fl oz
cauliflower sauce
(see page 20)

1 pheasant,
jointed and boned
by your butcher

75 ml/2½ fl oz
white wine

1 shallot, finely
chopped

10 g/¼ oz black
truffle, finely
chopped, plus
15 g/½ oz finely
sliced into 12

175 ml/6 fl oz
whipping cream

salt and freshly
ground white
pepper

150 g/5½ oz
fresh pasta dough
(see page 56)

2 tbsp olive oil

20 g/¾ oz butter

Suggested wine:
Cabernet
Sauvignon Pelago
Umani Ronchi,
1994, Marche

Both pheasant and black winter truffle are
at their best between mid-December and
mid-February. The light cauliflower sauce
complements these two strong tastes
beautifully. This is a great special occasion
dish for a winter party. If truffle is
unavailable, you could serve the tortelloni
with sautéed wild mushrooms such as porcini.

Prepare the cauliflower sauce and set aside. Do not whisk in the olive
oil until ready to serve. Roughly chop the pheasant leg meat, then put
it in a blender or food processor and pulse to a purée. Transfer to a
bowl. Heat the wine with the shallot until reduced by half, then strain
into the pheasant purée, discarding the shallot. Stir the chopped
truffle into the purée, then leave to cool and refrigerate for a few
minutes. Add the cream, stirring until smooth. Season.
Make the pasta dough and divide into 4 equal pieces. Pass it through the
pasta machine, finishing at the lowest setting, until you have 4 very
thin, almost transparent sheets (see page 56). Transfer to a lightly
floured surface. Make the tortelloni by following the method on page 57,
using the pheasant mixture as a filling.
Heat the olive oil with the butter and sauté the pheasant breasts for 3
minutes on each side until brown on the outside and pink inside. Remove
the skin and set aside to rest for 5 minutes. Slice the meat diagonally.
Cook the tortelloni in plenty of boiling salted water for 4-5 minutes,
then drain. Gently heat the cauliflower sauce and whisk in the olive oil
to finish.
Spoon the sauce around 4 warmed serving plates, add the tortelloni and
garnish with the sliced black truffle and the slices of breast meat.

67

6

Garganelli con salsa di broccoli e filetti di sogliola alla griglia

GARGANELLI PASTA WITH BROCCOLI SAUCE AND GRILLED DOVER SOLE

150 ml/¼ pint broccoli sauce (see page 20)

400 g/14 oz fresh pasta dough (see page 56)

8 Dover sole fillets, about 60-85 g/2¼-3 oz each, skinned

2 tbsp olive oil

salt

85 g/3 oz broccoli florets

50g/1¾ oz tomato concassée (1 tomato)

Suggested wine: Pinot Nero F. Haas Blauburgunder Cru Schweizer, 1996, Trentino Alto Adige

Garganelli is a shape of pasta that comes from the town of Ferrara and the surrounding region of Emilia Romagna. It resembles penne, but it is always handmade; you could use dried penne instead. If Dover sole is unavailable or too expensive, use red mullet fillets.

Prepare the broccoli sauce and set aside. Do not whisk in the olive oil until you are ready to serve.
Make the pasta dough and garganelli by following the methods on pages 56-7.
Heat a cast-iron ridged grill pan. Brush the Dover sole fillets with 1 tbsp olive oil and sprinkle with salt. Cut each fillet into 3 pieces and cook for 4 minutes on one side only.
Cook the garganelli in plenty of boiling salted water for 4-5 minutes, and the broccoli florets in a separate pan for 2 minutes until just tender. Drain the pasta and broccoli and toss together with 1 tbsp olive oil and the tomato concassée.
Gently heat the broccoli sauce and whisk in the olive oil to finish.
Spoon the sauce over 4 warmed soup plates, add the garganelli and broccoli mixture and top each serving with 6 pieces of Dover sole, grilled-side up.

❼

Stracci di pasta con coniglio e funghi di bosco

STRACCI PASTA WITH RABBIT AND WILD MUSHROOMS

1 whole rabbit, prepared for the oven, and 1 saddle

100 ml/3¹/₂ fl oz rabbit jus (see pages 17-18)

90 g/3¹/₄ oz butter

1 onion, finely diced

salt and white pepper

500 ml/18 fl oz rabbit stock (see page 17)

85 g/3 oz fresh spinach pasta dough (see pages 56-7)

85 g/3 oz fresh plain pasta dough (see page 56)

3 tbsp white wine

2 tbsp olive oil

125 g/4¹/₂ oz wild mushrooms, such as morels, chanterelles, pieds de mouton, ceps, sliced

Suggested wine: Pinot Nero Dell'Abazia Serafini e Vidotto, 1995, Veneto

The stracci in this warming autumnal dish are made from spinach pasta dough as well as plain dough. In Italy, meat is often cooked in its own fat over a long period of time to make a confit; here, the rabbit is cooked very gently in stock and a little butter for a lighter variation on a classic theme.

Ask your butcher to joint the rabbit and bone the saddles. Reserve the bones for making the jus. Cut the saddle meat into small pieces, about 1 cm/½ in x 1 cm/½ in.
Preheat the oven to 150°C/300°F/gas mark 2.
Heat 20 g/¾ oz butter in a pan and cook the diced onion for 3-4 min or until soft. In a roasting pan heat 35 g/1¼ oz butter, add the legs, season, and brown them all over. Add the softened onion, then pour in the rabbit stock to cover. Cover the pan with kitchen foil and cook in the oven for 40 minutes.
In the meantime make the pasta doughs and stracci, following the method on page 56-7. Set aside on a tray dusted with semolina flour and cover with a cloth.
Remove the rabbit legs from the oven and strip the meat from the bones. Discard the bones and set aside the meat, covering it and keeping it warm.
Heat 10 g/¼ oz butter in a pan, season the rabbit saddle meat and sauté for about 5 minutes - it should still be pink inside. Remove the meat from the pan and set aside. Pour off the butter from the pan and add the white wine to deglaze. Bring to the boil, add the rabbit jus and let it bubble for 2-3 minutes until slightly reduced. Whisk the remaining butter into the sauce, season to taste and stir in the strips of leg meat.
Heat 2 tbsp olive oil in another pan, add the mushrooms and cook for about 3 minutes, then add to the sauce, with any juices. Cook the stracci in boiling salted water for 1 minute until al dente. Drain and toss with the sauce.
Divide the pasta and sauce among 4 warmed serving plates and top with the rabbit saddle meat.

Pappardelle al ragu di lepre, cavolo nero

PAPPARDELLE WITH HARE SAUCE AND CAVOLO NERO

1 hare, prepared for the oven

3¹/₂ tbsp olive oil

85 g/3 oz Italian lard, cut into 1 cm/¹/₂ in cubes

2 carrots, cut into 1 cm/¹/₂ in cubes

200ml/7 fl oz red wine

400 ml/14 fl oz plum tomato coulis (about 10 tomatoes)

salt and white pepper

400 g/14 oz fresh pasta dough (see page 56)

500 g/1 lb 2 oz butter

3¹/₂ tbsp cognac

1 cavolo nero

THE MARINADE
1 carrot and 2 celery stalks, roughly chopped

1 onion, roughly chopped

1¹/₂ leeks, roughly chopped

5-6 bay leaves

500-600 ml/18 fl oz-1 pint red wine

Suggested wine: Barolo Cannubi Boschis Luciano Sandrone, 1991, Piemonte

This is my version of a famous Italian classic, and a very special winter dish. The sauce is made in the traditional way, but the meat for the garnish is cooked rare. The lard gives the meat a delicious flavour. I use Italian lard from Colonnata, but you could use ordinary lard if you have trouble finding this.

Ask your butcher to joint and bone the hare. You will be using the legs for the ragu and the saddle for the garnish. Put the leg meat in a dish together with all the marinade ingredients, making sure they are covered by the wine. Leave in the fridge overnight.

Strain the marinade, remove the meat and cut it into 1 cm/½ in cubes. Discard the vegetables and the wine. Heat 2½ tbsp olive oil with the lard in a flameproof casserole and add the cubed carrots. When the carrots start to colour add the marinaded meat and cook for 10-15 minutes. Add the wine and heat until slightly reduced, then add the tomato coulis and seasoning. Simmer gently for a further 40 minutes until reduced and thickened to a ragu.

Meanwhile make the pasta dough and pappardelle according to the methods on pages 56-7. Set aside on a tray dusted with semolina flour and cover with a cloth.

Preheat the oven to 180°C/350°F/gas mark 4. Cut each saddle loin in half. Clarify the butter (see page 188), then pour it into a casserole dish. Add the cognac and the 4 pieces of saddle loin. Cook in the oven for 4 minutes, then remove the hare. Cover and set aside to rest.

Trim the cavolo nero and blanch the leaves in boiling salted water for 3 minutes, then drain. Heat 1 tbsp olive oil in a pan and sauté the leaves for 1 minute.

Cook the pappardelle in plenty of boiling salted water for 3 minutes and gently warm the ragu. Drain the pasta and toss with the ragu. Slice the meat from the hare saddles into long strips.

Divide the pappardelle and sauce among 4 warmed serving plates and garnish with the sautéed leaves and the saddle meat.

Tagliolini al nero di seppia con broccoli

SQUID INK TAGLIOLINI WITH BROCCOLI

280 g/10 oz squid
ink pasta dough
(see page 56-7)

4 oysters

150 g/5^1/$_2$ oz
mussels

150 g/5^1/$_2$ oz
clams

3 tbsp olive oil

4 garlic cloves,
whole

4 parsley stalks

2 tbsp white wine

100 g/3^1/$_2$ oz
broccoli, cut
into florets

8 asparagus
stalks, tips
trimmed to
3 cm/1^1/$_4$ in

4 tomato petals
(see page 189),
sliced into
julienne strips

3 anchovies,
finely chopped

10 g/^{1}/$_4$ oz
capers, finely
chopped

1 tbsp olive oil

salt and white
pepper

^{1}/$_2$ shallot,
finely chopped

Suggested wine:
Cervaro Della
Sala, Antinori,
1997, Umbria

I usually serve this cold for a summer lunch, but if you prefer you can serve it hot - simply toss the cooked pasta with the shellfish juices over a gentle heat. The contrasting colours of the ingredients - jet black, green and red - make this a very attractive dish.

Make the squid ink pasta dough and tagliolini according to the methods on pages 56-7.

Carefully open the oysters with an oyster knife and reserve any juices. Scrub the mussels and clams thoroughly, removing any beards. Heat the olive oil in a pan then add the mussels and clams, together with the garlic and parsley stalks. After 2 minutes add the white wine and oyster juices. Cover the pan and cook for about 7 minutes or until all the shellfish are open. Discard any that do not open.

Take the open shellfish from the pan, remove the flesh from the shells and discard the shells. Strain the liquid from the pan through a chinois or fine-meshed sieve into a clean pan.

You may need to strain the liquid twice to get rid of any sand or grit.

Prepare three bowls of iced water. Cook the broccoli in plenty of boiling salted water for about 6 minutes until tender. Refresh in iced water and drain. Cook the asparagus tips for about 6 minutes until tender, then refresh and drain. Cook the tagliolini in plenty of salted boiling water for 3 minutes, refresh in iced water and drain.

Gently reheat the shellfish juices. Toss the tagliolini with the shellfish meat, tomatoes, anchovies and capers. Add the juices, the olive oil, seasoning and chopped shallot.

Divide among 4 warmed serving plates and top with the oysters.

Gnocchi di patate farciti ai carciofi, salsa di zenzero e vino bianco

POTATO GNOCCHI STUFFED WITH ARTICHOKES, WITH WHITE WINE AND GINGER SAUCE

lemon juice

7 globe
artichokes

500 ml/18 fl oz
olive oil, plus
1 tbsp

2 garlic cloves,
crushed

1 thyme sprig

75 ml/2½ fl oz
vegetable stock
(see page 17)

1 tbsp dry white
wine

200 g/7 oz
ricotta cheese

50 g/1¾ oz
Parmesan cheese

1 egg yolk,
beaten

salt and white
pepper

1 quantity
potato gnocchi
(see page 78)

THE SAUCE
about 450 g/1 lb
fresh root ginger

200 ml/⅓ pint
white wine

85 g/3 oz butter

Suggested wine:
Studio delle
Venezie Borgo del
Tiglio 1996
Friuli Venezia
Giulia

The gnocchi here are essentially the same as in the recipe for potato gnocchi with cherry tomatoes (see page 78). The only difference is that they are stuffed with a delicious filling of artichokes and ricotta.

Prepare a bowl of acidulated water (water with lemon juice) for the artichokes. Peel off the tough outer leaves until you reach the tender heart, then cut off the top third and scoop out the choke. Slice off a small amount of the green part at the bottom, then set aside 2 whole artichoke hearts to garnish. Slice the remaining 5 hearts horizontally. Put the slices in the water to stop them from turning brown.
Heat 1 tbsp oil in a pan and add the garlic and thyme. After 30 seconds add the artichoke slices. Heat the stock in a separate pan. Add the wine to the artichoke slices then once it has evaporated, add the hot stock. Cover the pan and cook for 10 minutes until the artichokes are tender. Strain the contents of the pan and discard the garlic and thyme. Blend the artichokes to a purée in a food processor, then pass through a chinois or fine-meshed sieve into a bowl. Leave to cool.
Stir the ricotta, Parmesan, egg yolk and seasoning into the artichoke purée. Store in the fridge while you make the gnocchi.
Boil the potatoes in their skins in plenty of boiling salted water. Drain and peel them. Purée the potatoes either through a fine sieve or with a potato ricer straight on to a wooden worksurface. Add the flour, egg, nutmeg, salt and pepper, using your hands to form a smooth dough. Divide into 4 or 5 pieces. Using a rolling pin roll each piece out on a lightly floured surface into a rectangular strip 20 cm x 7 cm/8 in x 2¾ in and about ½ cm/¼ in thick. Place teaspoons of filling along the length of 1 side of each piece of dough at 5 cm/2 in intervals, then carefully bring the other side over to enclose the filling. Using 1 side of a 5 cm/2 in round cutter, press out half-moon shapes without cutting through the folded side. Slice the 2 remaining artichoke hearts into fine julienne strips. Heat 500 ml/18 fl oz olive oil in a heavy-based pan to 180°C/350°F/gas mark 4, add the artichoke slices and fry for 3 minutes until golden, turning constantly.
To make the sauce, peel the ginger and grate it, then press it through a fine sieve to yield about 100 ml/3½ fl oz juice. Heat the wine in a pan until reduced by one-third. Add the ginger juice and reduce by half again. Cook the gnocchi in plenty of salted boiling water for 3 minutes. As soon as they start to rise to the surface, remove them from the water with a slotted spoon. Whisk the butter into the sauce, then remove from the heat. Add the gnocchi to the sauce, then divide immediately among 4 warmed serving plates. Garnish with the fried artichoke.

ⅠⅠ

Gnocchi di patate con pomodori ciliegia e triglie

POTATO GNOCCHI WITH CHERRY TOMATOES AND RED MULLET

4 tbsp olive oil

2 garlic cloves, crushed

1 shallot, finely chopped

1 small red chilli, deseeded and finely chopped

32 cherry tomatoes, quartered

8 red mullet fillets, about 40 g/1¾ oz each, skin on

salt and white pepper

4 basil leaves

THE GNOCCHI
200 g/7 oz waxy potatoes

85 g/3 oz plain flour

1 egg, beaten

pinch of nutmeg

salt and freshly ground white pepper

Suggested wine: Pinot Grigio Livio Felluga, 1997 Friuli Venezia Giulia

This lovely dish is extremely adaptable. Potato gnocchi are typical of the Veneto region and can be eaten simply tossed with butter or pesto sauce. For best results, use a waxy potato, and prepare the dough while the potatoes are still hot.

In a pan, warm 1 tbsp olive oil and add the garlic, shallot and chilli. Cook for 2-3 minutes until the garlic and shallots are translucent but not golden. Add the cherry tomatoes and cover the pan with a lid. Leave to cook over a low heat for 3-4 minutes.

Make the gnocchi. Boil the potatoes in their skins in plenty of boiling salted water. Drain them, then peel, protecting your hands with a cloth if necessary. Purée the potatoes either through a fine sieve or with a potato ricer straight on to a wooden worksurface. Add the flour, egg, nutmeg, salt and pepper. Using your hands work the egg and flour into the potato until you have a smooth dough. Divide the dough into 4 or 5 pieces. On a lightly floured surface roll each piece of dough with the palm of your hand to make long tubes about 1 cm/½ in in diameter. Place on a lightly floured surface and cut into ½ cm/¼ in lengths. To shape the gnocchi, slide each one down the prongs of a fork to make the mark of the fork on one side and the indent from your finger on the other. Cover and refrigerate while you cook the fish.

Heat 1 tbsp olive oil in a sauté pan, season the red mullet and cook skin-side down for 3 minutes until the skin is crispy. Turn over and cook on the other side for 1 minute. Once cooked, slice each fillet diagonally in half.

Remove the garlic from the tomato mixture. Crush the tomatoes with a wooden spoon and season to taste. Heat the sauce gently, then tear the basil into strips and add to the tomatoes. Whisk 2 tbsp olive oil into the sauce to finish.

Cook the gnocchi in boiling salted water for about 1 minute or until they rise to the surface.

Drain the gnocchi and toss immediately with the tomato sauce. Serve the gnocchi and sauce in individual soup bowls and top each serving with 4 pieces of red mullet.

masterclass 3: risotto
riso mantecato allo zafferano

SAFFRON RISOTTO

500 ml/18 fl oz
chicken stock
(see page 17)

1 onion, very
finely chopped

50 g/1³/₄ oz
butter

320 g/11 oz
vialone nano rice

100 ml/3¹/₂ fl oz
dry white wine

pinch of saffron

salt and white
pepper

50 g/1³/₄ oz acid
butter (see page
21), or
equivalent
ordinary butter
and a few drops
white wine
vinegar

60 g/2 oz
Parmesan cheese,
grated

Suggested wine:
Chardonnay Rossy
Bass A. Gaja,
1997, Piemonte

Risotto should be made exclusively with plump, round-grain Italian rice, which is able to absorb a great deal of liquid. My preference is to use vialone nano, a semi-fino rice, but you can use arborio or carnaroli. There are basically five stages to cooking a risotto. First is *il soffrito*, when a base of onions is gently fried in butter or olive oil. This is followed by *la tostatura*, when the uncooked rice is heated in the **soffritto** to coat the grains in fat and partially seal them. Then comes *la cottura*, or the cooking stage, when the rice is simmered in stock. The stock should always be of good quality, and it should be kept hot in a separate pan so that it does not lower the temperature when added to the rice.

At this stage the rice releases enough starch to make a thick, creamy sauce and begins really to soak up the liquid. The penultimate stage is *all' onda*, when the rice has cooked to the perfect al dente consistency; it should, when the pan is jerked sharply, roll like a wave (*onda*) falling on the shore. The final stage is *mantecare,* in which you take the pan off the stove and stir in the acid butter. I use this butter in my risotto recipes to sharpen the flavour, but it's not essential. However, if you like a touch of acidity, as I do, but don't want to prepare the butter especially, stir in a few drops of wine vinegar. Unless your risotto contains seafood, this is when you would stir in the Parmesan. In the restaurant, I always serve my risotto on a flat plate.

1 Pour the stock into a pan and keep it simmering over a low heat while you prepare the risotto.

2 *Il soffrito*. In a risotto pan - you can use a tall-sided, heavy-bottomed casserole but never a frying pan, as it disperses moisture too quickly - cook the chopped onion with a small knob of the butter (about 20 g/¾ oz) over a medium heat until it starts to turn yellow and has become sweet and soft.

3 *La tostatura*. Now add the rice in a stream and stir with a wooden spoon for about 30 seconds until the rice is well coated with the butter and has become glossy and opaque.

4 *La cottura*. Raise the heat slightly under the rice. Pour over the white wine and leave to cook while the wine boils away completely. Do not stir the rice at this stage: if you stir before it has had a chance to boil, the grains will become cooked on the outside but not on the inside. Once the wine has evaporated add 2 ladles of hot stock. Stir gently with a wooden spoon to prevent the rice sticking to the pan.

5 Crush the saffron with the back of a spoon and add it to the rice. Once the stock has reduced continue to add more stock to the pan,

one ladle at a time, until the rice is cooked, making sure you don't drown it. The cooking time should be about 17 minutes, by which time the rice grains should have swollen to about twice their original size. It's a good idea to start tasting after about 12 minutes to see if the rice is al dente. Season with salt and pepper. Add only enough liquid now to keep the sauce creamy and slightly runny. If you run out of stock, use boiling water.

6 *All 'onda*. Check that the rice is the right consistency by shaking the pan firmly. This should produce a wave across the surface of the risotto.

7 *Mantecare*. When the rice is cooked remove it immediately from the heat and gently stir in the remaining butter and acid butter, or ordinary butter and wine vinegar. Stir in the grated Parmesan and serve immediately, on warmed flat plates.

Riso mantecato alle cappesante e asparagi

RISOTTO WITH SCALLOPS AND ASPARAGUS

8 large scallops, cleaned and roes removed

8 asparagus stalks

500 ml/18 fl oz vegetable stock (see page 17)

50 g/1³/₄ oz butter

20 g/1³/₄ oz onion, finely chopped

320 g/11 oz vialone nano rice

100 ml/3¹/₂ fl oz white wine

1 tbsp olive oil

50 g/1³/₄ oz acid butter (see page 21), or equivalent ordinary butter and a few drops white wine vinegar

salt and white pepper

Suggested wine: Sauvignon St. Valentin. K.G.T. St Michael Eppan, 1997, Trentino Alto Adige

In this recipe the combination of land and sea works superbly. You need only cook the scallops on one side because when you place the uncooked side over the rice the heat from the rice will finish the cooking.

First, prepare the scallops and the asparagus. Slice the scallops in half horizontally to make two discs. Trim the asparagus then cut the tips to about 4-5 cm/1¹/₂-2 in long and set aside. Chop the rest of the asparagus into small pieces.

Put the stock in a pan and keep it simmering over a low heat while you prepare the risotto. Heat 20 g/³/₄ oz of the butter in a risotto pan or a tall-sided, heavy-bottomed casserole and cook the chopped onion over a medium heat until soft. Add the rice and chopped asparagus and stir with a wooden spoon until well coated with the butter. Raise the heat slightly, then add the wine. Wait until the wine has evaporated - do not stir the rice - and then add 2 ladlesful of the hot stock. Stir the rice gently to prevent it from sticking to the pan. Continue to add stock, 1 ladle at a time, until the rice is tender - this should take about 17 minutes. When ready, the consistency of the rice should be *all'onda* (see page 80).

Meanwhile cook the asparagus tips in boiling salted water for 2-3 minutes then drain. Heat the olive oil in a pan and cook the scallops briefly on one side only for about 1 minute.

When the rice is cooked remove it from the heat and gently stir in the remaining butter and the acid butter or ordinary butter and wine vinegar. Season to taste.

Divide the risotto among 4 warmed flat plates and place 4 scallop halves over each serving, uncooked-side down. Arrange 4 asparagus tips between the halves.

⓭

Riso mantecato con fegatini di pollo e formaggio di capra

RISOTTO WITH CHICKEN LIVERS AND GOAT'S CHEESE

500 ml/18 fl oz
chicken stock
(see page 17)

50 g/1³/₄ oz
butter

20 g/³/₄ oz
onion, finely
chopped

320 g/11 oz
vialone nano rice

100 ml/3¹/₂ fl oz
white wine

12 chicken
livers, cleaned

3 tbsp madeira

1 tbsp chicken
jus (see pages
17-18)

salt and white
pepper

25 g/1 oz
Parmesan cheese,
grated

50 g/1³/₄ oz acid
butter (see page
21), or
equivalent
ordinary butter
and a few drops
white wine
vinegar

85 g/3 oz fresh
goat's cheese

Suggested wine:
Cabernet
Sauvignon
Romigberg A.
Lageder, 1993,
Trentino Alto
Adige

This is a delicious, rich-tasting risotto.
It's also very easy to prepare.

Put the stock in a pan and keep it simmering over a low heat while you prepare the risotto.
Heat 20 g/³/₄ oz of the butter in a risotto pan or a tall-sided, heavy-bottomed casserole and cook the chopped onion over a medium heat until soft. Add the rice and stir with a wooden spoon until it is well coated with the butter. Raise the heat slightly, then add the wine. Wait until the wine has evaporated - do not stir the rice - and then add 2 ladlesful of the hot stock. Stir the rice gently to prevent it from sticking to the pan. Continue to add stock, 1 ladle at a time, until the rice is tender - this should take about 17 minutes. When ready, the consistency of the rice should be all'onda (see page 80).
In a separate pan heat 20 g/³/₄ oz of the butter and cook the chicken livers until browned but still pink inside - about 3 minutes on each side. Remove the livers from the pan and set aside. Pour off the fat from the pan and add the madeira, then bring to a simmer and reduce by three-quarters. Add the chicken jus and heat until the liquid has reduced by half. Stir in 10 g/¼ oz butter to finish the sauce and season to taste.
Remove the rice from the heat then gently stir in the remaining butter and acid butter or ordinary butter and wine vinegar, the Parmesan, a little more seasoning and the goat's cheese.
Slice the chicken livers in half horizontally. Divide the risotto among 4 warmed flat plates and arrange the chicken livers on top. Spoon the sauce over the livers, or serve it separately.

⑭

Riso mantecato alle alzavole, menta e funghi porcini

RISOTTO WITH TEAL, MINT AND WILD MUSHROOMS

4 teal or duck,
prepared for the
oven, or 8 teal
or duck breasts

500 ml/18 fl oz
chicken stock
(see page 17)

60 g/2 oz butter

20 g/³/₄ oz onion,
finely chopped

320 g/11 oz
vialone nano rice

100 ml/3¹/₂ fl oz
red wine

2 tbsp olive oil

85 g/3 oz
porcini, cleaned
and sliced

2 garlic cloves

2 tbsp teal,
duck or chicken
jus (see pages
17-18)

50 g/1³/₄ oz acid
butter (see page
21), or
equivalent
ordinary butter
and a few drops
white wine
vinegar

6 mint leaves,
finely sliced
into julienne
strips

40 g/1¹/₂ oz
Parmesan cheese,
grated

salt and white
pepper

Suggested wine:
Barolo Bussia
Parusso, 1985,
Piemonte

This is probably my favourite risotto.
The addition of mint at the very end of the
recipe gives the dish a wonderfully fresh
flavour. You can use duck instead of teal,
and any combination of wild mushrooms if
porcini are not available.

If you're using whole birds, ask your butcher to joint them and bone the
breasts. Reserve the carcass if you are making the jus.

Put the stock in a pan and keep it simmering over a low heat while you
prepare the risotto. Heat 20 g/³/₄ oz of the butter in a risotto pan or a
tall-sided, heavy-bottomed casserole and cook the chopped onion over a
medium heat until soft. Add the rice and stir with a wooden spoon until
it is well coated with the butter. Raise the heat slightly, then add the
wine. Wait until the wine has evaporated - do not stir the rice - and
then add 2 ladlesful of the hot stock. Stir the rice gently to prevent
it from sticking to the pan. Continue to add stock, 1 ladle at a time,
until the rice is tender - this should take about 17 minutes. When
ready, the consistency of the rice should be *all'onda* (see page 80).

Meanwhile heat 1 tbsp olive oil in a pan and sauté the breasts for 2
minutes on each side until brown on the outside and pink in the middle.
Cover and set aside to rest.

Heat 1 tbsp olive oil in another pan, add the mushrooms and garlic and
sauté for 2-3 minutes until tender. Reserve any juices given out. Gently
heat the jus and whisk in 10 g/¹/₄ oz butter to finish. When the rice is
cooked remove it from the heat and gently stir in the remaining butter
and the acid butter or ordinary butter and wine vinegar, together with
the mushrooms, mint and parmesan. Season to taste.

Slice each breast diagonally into 2 pieces. Divide the risotto among 4
warmed flat plates, arrange the breast slices on top, and spoon over the
sauce or serve it separately.

masterclass 4: consommé

Makes 3 l/5¼ pints

300 g/9½ oz chicken breast, roughly chopped

150 g/5½ oz carrots, roughly chopped

100 g/3½ oz celery, roughly chopped

100 g/3½ oz onions, roughly chopped

3 button mushrooms, halved

½ fennel bulb, roughly chopped

small bunch of flat-leaf parsley

10 egg whites

75 g/2¾ oz salt

5 l/8¾ pints chicken stock (page 17)

about 15-20 ice cubes

Consommé is a clarified stock with a very concentrated flavour. It can be drunk as it is, as a clear, pure soup, or used as a base for other soups and sauces. It is made with egg whites, which clarify the liquid by forming a crust over the top and absorbing any impurities. You can make consommé with either meat or fish. For example, if you want to make a fish consommé, substitute fish stock or shellfish stock (see page 16) and use the flesh from a white fish such as sole or cod, or langoustines if you prefer something a little more luxurious. Beef consommé should be made with beef stock, pheasant consommé with pheasant stock, and so on. Consommé will keep for three to four days in the fridge, or it can be frozen for up to six months. You will need a large deep pan or stock pan; if you don't have one large enough, halve the quantities given in this recipe.

1 Place all the ingredients apart from the egg whites, salt, stock and ice cubes in a food processor and chop into small pieces — they don't need to be too fine. You may need to do this in batches. Transfer the mixture to a large mixing bowl.

88

2 Whisk the egg whites briefly with the salt to break them up. Pour the egg mixture over the chopped vegetables and chicken breast, add the ice cubes and mix together.

3 Pour the stock into a large stock pan and add the contents of the mixing bowl. Bring very slowly to simmering point over a moderate heat, stirring with a wooden spoon. Be careful not to let it boil.

4 Just before it reaches boiling point, lower the heat until the liquid is at the gentlest simmer possible. Leave to simmer on a very low heat for 30-45 minutes. During this time the egg whites will gradually form a crust over the liquid. This will break up in places to allow bubbles to surface.

Do not allow the liquid to boil at any point — if the heat is too high the egg crust will break up too much and merge with the liquid.

5 Carefully remove the pan from the heat and leave to settle for 30 minutes.

6 Strain the consommé through a chinois or fine-meshed sieve, discarding the egg crust. Allow to cool, then store in the fridge in a covered container until needed. When you want to use the consommé, reheat it gently and season to taste.

Consommé di pollo e cappesante

CHICKEN CONSOMME WITH SCALLOPS

1 l/1³/₄ pints
chicken consommé
(see page 88)

4 scallops, cleaned
and roes removed

1 tbsp soy sauce

small bunch of
chives

zest of 1 unwaxed
lemon, finely
sliced into strips

8 shiitake
mushrooms, finely
sliced

THE TORTELLINI
20g/³/₄ oz butter

1 shallot, finely
chopped

400 g/14 oz chicken
breast, cubed

1 tbsp cognac

100 g/3¹/₂ oz cooked
ham, chopped

100 g/3¹/₂ oz
ricotta cheese

20 g/³/₄ oz grated
Parmesan

1 egg yolk

pinch of grated
nutmeg

salt and white
pepper

100 g/3¹/₂ oz fresh
pasta dough (see
page 56)

Suggested wine:
Chardonnay Planeta,
1997, Sicilia

The authentic recipe for chicken tortellini comes from my home town of Lugo di Romagna. Scuaqquarone - a fresh, unpasteurised local cheese that you won't find in this country is used there, but I have substituted ricotta. There is no need to cook the scallops - the heat of the consommé will gently cook them through once you are ready to serve. You can freeze any tortellini you don't use and serve them on another occasion with a fresh pasta sauce. Cook them straight from frozen for 1 minute longer.

Prepare the consommé (see page 88).
Prepare the filling for the tortellini. In a sauté pan melt the butter, add the shallot then when it starts to colour add the chicken breast and cook for about 2 minutes. Add the cognac and allow to evaporate. Remove the chicken from the pan and place in a processor with the ham and ricotta. Blend to a purée then transfer to a bowl. Stir in the Parmesan, egg yolk, nutmeg and seasoning.
Prepare the pasta dough and pass through the pasta machine, finishing at the lowest setting, until you have a very thin, almost transparent sheet (see page 56). Place on a lightly floured surface and, using a pastry cutter, cut into squares 2¹/₂ x 2¹/₂ cm/1 x 1 in. Make the tortellini according to the method on page 57, using the chicken mixture as a filling. Set aside on a tray dusted with semolina flour in a cool place until ready to cook.
Slice each scallop horizontally into 5-6 thin discs and place in a shallow bowl or container. Drizzle the soy sauce over the scallops and leave to marinate for 5-10 minutes.
Trim the chives to about 2¹/₂ cm/1 in long and reserve. Blanch the lemon zest 3 times for a few seconds each time and set aside.
Cook the tortellini in plenty of boiling salted water for 5-7 minutes, then drain.
While they are cooking, heat the chicken consommé.
Divide the scallops among 4 warmed serving plates, sprinkle over the chives, mushrooms and lemon zest, then add the tortellini. Pour the consommé over the top, or serve it separately from a tureen.

Crema di zucca

PUMPKIN SOUP

1 tbsp olive oil

1 large onion, finely chopped

1 garlic clove, crushed

600 g/1 lb 5 oz peeled pumpkin flesh, diced

300 ml/½ pint vegetable stock (see page 17)

salt and white pepper

Suggested wine: Tocai Friulano Borgo Magredo, 1998, Friuli Venezia Giulia

A classic way to serve this delicious and very simple autumnal soup is with Amaretti biscuits, but I also like to serve it with steamed Dover sole. Don't be surprised by the small amount of stock used in this recipe - the pumpkin releases a lot of liquid.

Heat the olive oil in a pan and add the onion and garlic. When they start to colour add the diced pumpkin and cook over a medium heat for 10 minutes until tender.
Heat the stock in a separate pan.
Add the hot stock to the pumpkin, bring to the boil, then reduce the heat and simmer for 30-40 minutes. Season to taste. Pass the soup through a chinois or fine-meshed sieve before serving.

Crema fredda di piselli con astice e piccione

COLD PEA SOUP WITH LOBSTER AND PIGEON

2 pigeons,
prepared for the
oven

500 ml/18 fl oz
pea sauce (see
page 19)

40 g/1¹/₂ oz
butter

1 tbsp olive oil

1 l/1³/₄ pints
court-bouillon
(see page 16)

2 live lobsters,
about 350-
400 g/12-14 oz

100 ml/3¹/₂ fl oz
pigeon or chicken
jus (see page 17)

salt and white
pepper

Suggested wine:
Pinot Bianco
Weisburgunder F.
Haas 1996
Trentino Alto
Adige

This dish uses a classic combination of flavours. My inspiration comes from a recipe devised by Gualtiero Marchesi, who serves lobster and roast pigeon with pigeon ravioli. I've used the same ingredients, but instead of ravioli, I've added a delicious pea soup. I like the soup to be chilled, but you can serve it hot if you prefer.

Ask your butcher to joint the pigeons and bone the pigeon breasts, reserving the carcass if you are making the jus.
Prepare the pea sauce, adjusting the consistency by adding more or less court-bouillon, as desired. Allow to cool, then place in the fridge for 30 minutes to 1 hour until chilled.
Melt half the butter in a sauté pan together with the olive oil. Add the pigeon legs and the breasts, skin-side down. Season the meat with salt and pepper and cook the breasts for 1-2 minutes on each side, leaving the meat pink inside. Remove the breasts from the pan then cook the legs for another 2 minutes until the skin is crisp. Cover and set aside.
Heat the court-bouillon in a large pan. To kill the lobsters, lay each one stomach downwards on the worksurface, then pierce through the crossmark on the skull with the tip of a large sharp knife. Plunge the lobsters in the court-bouillon and cook for 4-6 minutes, depending on size. Remove from the court-bouillon and set aside to cool. Once the lobsters are cool enough to handle remove the claws and head. Open the claws with kitchen scissors and remove the meat, preferably in 1 piece. Cut the tails in half lengthways, scoop out the meat from the shell and slice each half into 3 pieces.
Put the jus in a pan and heat until reduced by half. Whisk in the rest of the butter to finish.
Season the chilled soup to taste, then divide among 4 soup plates. Arrange the meat from 1 lobster half-tail and the meat from 1 claw on each plate. Slice the pigeon breast meat and arrange 3 slices and 1 pigeon leg per person next to the lobster. Spoon a little of the sauce around.

Crema di sedano e gorgonzola con ravioli di pollo e tartufo nero

---

CREAM OF CELERY AND GORGONZOLA WITH CHICKEN AND BLACK TRUFFLE RAVIOLI

1 tbsp olive oil

1 onion finely cut

400 g/14 oz celery, finely diced

400 g/14 oz celeriac, finely diced

200 ml/7 fl oz chicken stock (see page 17)

200 ml/7 fl oz whipping cream

salt and white pepper

250 g/9 oz Gorgonzola cheese

about 35 g/1¼ oz black truffle, sliced into 12 (optional)

THE RAVIOLI
400 g/14 oz chicken breast

100 ml/3½ fl oz whipping cream

1 tbsp olive oil

1 shallot, finely chopped

2 tbsp madeira

10 g/¼ oz black truffle, finely chopped (optional)

salt and white pepper

100 g/3½ oz fresh pasta dough (see page 56)

Suggested wine: Rosso dell'Abazia Serafini e Vidotto, 1996, Veneto

This soup includes chicken ravioli similar to the tortellini in the recipe for chicken consommé with scallops (see page 90), but this time the filling has a slightly more delicate flavour to complement the Gorgonzola cheese, which gradually melts with the heat of the soup. You can freeze any ravioli you don't use and serve them on another occasion with a fresh pasta sauce. Cook them straight from frozen for 1 minute longer than usual.

First prepare the ravioli filling. Purée the chicken breast in a blender (for a really smooth texture pass it through a chinois or fine-meshed sieve into a bowl). Stir in the cream and place in the fridge to chill. Heat 1 tbsp olive oil in a pan and add the shallot. Sauté for 30 seconds, then add the madeira. Heat gently, then remove from the heat and leave to cool. Stir the madeira and shallot into the chicken and cream purée, then add the chopped truffle and seasoning.

Make the pasta dough and divide into 8 pieces. Pass it through the pasta machine, finishing at the lowest setting, until you have 8 very thin, almost transparent sheets (see page 56). Transfer to a lightly floured surface. Using a teaspoon, place small mounds of the chicken filling along one half of the pasta sheet, spacing them evenly in rows and leaving a gap of 5 cm/2 in between each mound, and 2-3 cm/¾-1 in at each edge. Bring the other half of the pasta sheet over the first half to cover the filling and press carefully around the edges to remove any air. Cut the ravioli into 5 x 5 cm/2 x 2 in squares using a pastry cutter.

To make the soup, heat the olive oil in a pan, add the onion and cook until it starts to colour. Add the celery and celeriac and sauté for 5 minutes. Bring the stock and the cream to the boil in a separate pan, then pour over the celery and celeriac. Cook over a gentle heat for 30 minutes. Purée the mixture in a blender, then pass through a chinois or fine-meshed sieve and season to taste.

Cook the ravioli in plenty of boiling salted water for 5 minutes until tender. Gently reheat the soup.

Place 3 ravioli on each warmed serving plate, then place teaspoonfuls of Gorgonzola between the ravioli. Place the sliced truffle (if using) on top of the Gorgonzola and pour the soup over.

Fish and shellfish

Fritto misto di pesce

MIXED FRIED FISH

8 oysters

4 scallops, cleaned and roes removed

8 langoustines, shelled and deveined

4 sole fillets, about 70 g/2¹/₂ oz each, skinned

4 red mullet fillets, about 50 g/8¹/₂ oz each, skin on

15 g/¹/₂ oz black truffle, sliced into 8 pieces

2 l/3¹/₂ pints olive oil, plus 3 tbsp

20 basil leaves

150 g/5¹/₂ oz fresh breadcrumbs

1 rosemary sprig, finely chopped

2 eggs

150 g/5¹/₂ oz clarified butter

85 ml/3 fl oz sweet-and-sour sauce (see page 21)

1 tbsp fish stock (see page 16)

THE TEMPURA
200 g/7 oz plain flour

20 g/³/₄ oz cornflour

10 g/¹/₄ oz bicarbonate of soda

pinch of salt

Suggested wine: Le Grance Caparzo, 1995, Toscana

You can find this dish all around the coast of Italy, made in different ways with different kinds of fish, depending on what is available from the market. Adapt the recipe to suit whichever fish you like - cod, for example, might replace sole - but try to ensure that you have a good range of textures.

Prepare the fish and shellfish. Open the oysters using an oyster knife. Slice each scallop horizontally into 3. Take 3 scallop slices and 2 truffle slices and thread them alternately on to a cocktail stick, starting and ending with a scallop slice. Repeat to make 4 skewers in total.

Prepare the tempura. Have 175 ml/6 fl oz iced water ready. Make sure the water is really cold, as this helps keep the batter crust crispier for longer. Sieve the flour into a bowl with the cornflour, bicarbonate of soda and salt. Gradually add the iced water, whisking gently as you pour it in, until you have a smooth paste. If there are any lumps pass the batter through a chinois or fine-meshed sieve.

Pulse 12 basil leaves and 3 tbsp olive oil in a blender to make a basil purée. Divide the tempura into 2 batches and stir the purée into one batch. Put half the breadcrumbs in a bowl, and the other half in another bowl with the rosemary. Whisk the eggs in a third bowl. You will need two separate deep frying pans. Pour half the oil into one pan and heat to 180-200°C/350-400°F/gas mark 4-6. Spear the oysters with a cocktail stick, dip each one in the basil tempura, then slide it off the stick into the oil. Fry for 3-4 minutes until crispy. Next, spear the langoustines, dip in the plain tempura and fry for 3-4 minutes until golden. Place the oysters and langoustines on a plate lined with kitchen paper. Briefly fry 8 basil leaves in the oil until crisp, lift out of the oil with a slotted spoon and set aside. Heat the remaining oil in the second pan until the temperature reaches 140-150°C/275-300°F/gas mark 1-2. Dip the fillets of sole and the scallop skewers first in the egg and then in the breadcrumbs, until well coated. Fry the fillets and skewers in the oil 2 pieces at a time transferring them to a plate lined with kitchen paper. Clarify the butter (see page 188). Heat the clarified butter in a pan and halve the red mullet fillets. Dip the fillet halves first in the egg and then in the breadcrumb mixture. Fry in the butter for 3-4 minutes until golden. Remove to a plate lined with kitchen paper. Gently warm the sweet-and-sour sauce with the fish stock. Arrange all the fish on a plate lined with a paper doily. Remove the cocktail sticks from the scallop skewers. Drizzle over the sweet-and-sour sauce and garnish with the fried basil leaves.

❷

Branzino arrosto, patate saltate, pomodori, olive e capperi

ROASTED FILLET OF SEABASS WITH SAUTEED POTATOES, TOMATOES, OLIVES AND CAPERS

6 large potatoes, such as King Edward or Cyprus

4 tbsp olive oil

40 g/5 oz butter

zest of 1/2 unwaxed lemon

6 Italian plum tomatoes, finely sliced into fine julienne strips

8 black olives, pitted

24 capers, rinsed

4 garlic cloves, crushed

4 basil leaves

thyme sprig

250 ml/9 fl oz fish stock (see page 16)

100 ml/3½ fl oz white wine

salt

4 seabass fillets, each about 175 g/6 oz, skin on

chervil, to garnish

Suggested wine: Pinot Bianco Cantine Terlano, 1988, Trentino Alto Adige

This recipe reminds me of the south of Italy, where capers, olives and tomatoes flourish under the bright Mediterranean sun. Make sure you blanch the potatoes first before frying them: the way they are cooked is essential to the success of this dish.

Blanch the potatoes in their skins in boiling salted water. Drain, allow to cool slightly, and then remove the skins. Cut the potatoes into slices 1/2 cm/1/4 in thick. Heat 1 tbsp olive oil with the butter in a pan and gently fry the potato slices until crisp and golden. Remove to a plate lined with kitchen paper.

Blanch the lemon zest for 2 minutes in boiling water until tender. Remove, allow to cool slightly, then chop into small pieces. Preheat the oven to 180°C/350°F/gas mark 4. Combine the tomatoes, olives, capers, garlic, basil, thyme, lemon zest, stock, wine, 1 tbsp olive oil and salt in a baking tray. Cook in the oven for 5 minutes until the tomatoes are tender. Remove half the tomatoes from the pan and set aside, then place the pan on the stove over a medium heat and simmer gently for 2 or 3 minutes until the mixture has reduced and thickened.

Meanwhile season the seabass, then heat 1 tbsp olive oil in a sauté pan and cook the fillets, skin-side down, for 6-8 minutes or until the skin is crispy.

Strain the sauce, then whisk in 1 tbsp olive oil to emulsify it.

Make sure you have whisked the olive oil thoroughly into the reduced sauce or it may separate.

Divide the potato slices among 4 warmed serving plates and place the reserved tomatoes on top, then the seabass fillets. Drizzle the sauce around the fish. Garnish with chervil.

3

Filleto di rombo al sale, spinaci saltati e salsa leggera di pomodoro

---

FILLET OF TURBOT COOKED IN A SEA-SALT CRUST, WITH SAUTEED SPINACH AND TOMATO SALSA

4 turbot fillets, about 175-200 g/6-7 oz each, skin on

50 g/1³/₄ oz rock or sea salt

400 g/14 oz spinach

50 g/1³/₄ oz butter

THE SAUCE
4 tomatoes, peeled and roughly chopped

50 g/1³/₄ oz tomato concassée (1 tomato)

20 black olives, finely sliced into julienne strips

20 capers, rinsed

100 ml/3¹/₂ fl oz white wine

1 tbsp balsamic vinegar

4 tbsp olive oil

salt and white pepper

leaves from 4 oregano sprigs

Suggested wine: Franciacorta Bianco E. Gatti, 1997, Lombardia

The sea salt covering the skin of the turbot allows it to cook nice and slowly, as well as subtly flavouring the fish throughout the cooking process. Make sure you cook the fish at the last minute and remove the skin and all the salt before serving.

First, make the sauce. Pulse the chopped tomatoes in a food processor, then pass through a chinois or fine-meshed sieve on to a plate lined with muslin. Tie into a small bundle and suspend from the handle of a wooden spoon over a bowl. Leave for 1 hour.
Put the tomato purée in a pan and add the tomato concassée, olives, capers, wine, vinegar, olive oil and seasoning.
Preheat the grill to medium high. Place the turbot pieces on a large baking sheet. Press the salt into the skin side of each piece then grill, skin-side up, for 8 minutes. Cover and set aside.
Meanwhile wash the spinach and drain it well. Heat the butter in a pan and sauté the spinach for 4 minutes.
Warm the sauce gently.

Don't let the sauce boil or it may separate.

Then add the oregano leaves.
Remove the skin and all the salt from the turbot pieces.
Divide the sautéed spinach among 4 warmed serving plates and place the turbot on top. Spoon the sauce around the fish and serve.

asparagus, broad beans and peas

2 tbsp extra virgin olive oil

35 g/1¹/₄ oz smoked pancetta or bacon, finely sliced

2 spring onions, finely chopped

100 ml/3¹/₂ fl oz chicken stock (see page 17)

salt and white pepper

100 g/3¹/₂ oz butter

4 monkfish fillets, each about 125 g/4¹/₂ oz, skinned

4 English lettuce leaves, finely sliced into julienne strips

white wine vinegar, for poaching

12 quail's eggs

40 g/1¹/₂ oz black truffle, grated (optional)

Suggested wine: Riesling Collio Schioppetto, 1998, Fricili Venezia

it absorbs all the flavours
as well as giving out its own delicious juices.
You should eat the quail's eggs at the very
end, as their delicate taste cleanses the palate.

Prepare the vegetables. Cut the turnips and carrots in half, or quarter them if they are large. Trim the asparagus and slice into pieces.
Prepare a bowl of iced water. Blanch all the vegetables separately in boiling water for 1-2 minutes, refresh in iced water and drain.
Heat 1 tbsp olive oil in a pan and gently sauté the pancetta with the chopped spring onions for 2-3 minutes. Add the vegetables and stock and season.
In a sauté pan, heat 15 g/¹/₂ oz butter with 1 tbsp olive oil. Season the monkfish fillets and sauté for 2 minutes on each side. Remove them from the pan, slice each one into 4 or 5 pieces then transfer them to the pan containing the stock and vegetables. Cook over medium heat for another 4-5 minutes.
Add the lettuce and whisk in the remaining butter.
Bring a pan of water to a gentle simmer and add a few drops of white wine vinegar. Crack the quail's eggs into the water and poach for 30 seconds, then carefully remove them with a slotted spoon and set aside on a plate lined with paper towels.
Divide the vegetables and sauce among 4 warmed serving plates and place the monkfish pieces on top. Carefully roll each quail's egg in the grated black truffle (if using) and arrange 3 of them around each serving.

❺

Coda di rospo farcita, salsa al peperoni rossi, tagliolini al nero di seppia

MONKFISH WITH RED PEPPER SAUCE AND SQUID INK TAGLIOLINI

150 g/5½ oz
squid ink
pasta dough
(see page 56)

4 tbsp olive oil

½ onion, finely
chopped

3 garlic cloves,
crushed

450 g/1 lb red
pepper, deseeded
and roughly
chopped

225 g/8 oz
tomatoes, roughly
chopped

salt and white
pepper

100 ml/3½ fl oz
vegetable stock

20 g/¾ oz salted
butter, softened

700 g/1 lb 10 oz
monkfish,
filleted and cut
into portions
about 175 g/6 oz
each, skinned

50 g/1¾ oz black
truffle, cut into
little batons

20 g/¾ oz
unsalted butter

24 spring onions,
trimmed

Suggested wine:
Pinot Nero
Vigneto S. Urbano
1996 Hofstatter
Trentino Alto
Adige

This colourful dish combines the delicate flavour of monkfish with a subtly sweet red pepper sauce.

Make the squid ink pasta dough and tagliolini by following the methods on pages 56-7. Set aside on a tray dusted with semolina flour and cover with a cloth until ready to cook.
To make the sauce, heat 1 tbsp olive oil in a pan and add the onion and garlic. When they start to colour add the red pepper and tomatoes, season and cook for 10 more minutes. Meanwhile gently heat the vegetable stock in a separate pan.
Add the hot stock to the peppers and tomatoes and cook for another 20 minutes. Remove the garlic, transfer to a blender and pulse to a purée, then pass through a chinois or fine-meshed sieve into a clean pan.
Take 4 pieces of kitchen foil 15 x 25 cm/6 x 10 in and grease them with the softened butter. Using a sharp knife make a slit along the edge of each monkfish fillet to make a pocket. Push a little of the truffle into the pocket. Place each monkfish piece on the centre of a piece of foil and wrap the foil tightly round the fish.
Preheat the oven to 170°C/325°F/gas mark 3. Heat 1 tbsp olive oil and 20 g/¾ oz unsalted butter in a pan and place the monkfish pieces, wrapped in foil, in the oil and butter. Heat for 2 minutes, then place in the oven for 6-8 minutes, depending on the thickness of the pieces. Remove from the oven and let the fish rest for 5-10 minutes, still wrapped in foil.
Blanch the spring onions for 2 minutes and cook the tagliolini for 2 minutes in plenty of boiling salted water. Drain, then briefly sauté the pasta with 1 tbsp olive oil.
Gently heat the sauce and whisk in 1 tbsp olive oil to finish.
Spoon the sauce around the 4 warmed serving plates and place the tagliolini on top. Unwrap the monkfish, cut the pieces into thick slices and arrance them around the pasta. Garnish with the spring onions.

Salmone confit, salsa al cavolo nero, vegetali autunnali

SALMON CONFIT WITH BLACK CABBAGE SAUCE AND AUTUMN VEGETABLES

300 ml/$\frac{1}{2}$ pint cavolo nero sauce (see page 20)

70 g/$2\frac{1}{2}$ oz baby turnips, quartered

70 g/$2\frac{1}{2}$ oz broccoli, cut into florets

70 g/$2\frac{1}{2}$ oz mange-touts, halved

70 g/$2\frac{1}{2}$ oz baby carrots, halved

70 g/$2\frac{1}{2}$ oz new potatoes, halved

3 tbsp olive oil plus 1.5 l/$2\frac{3}{4}$ pints olive oil, for cooking the salmon

salt and white pepper

4 x 175 g/6 oz salmon fillets, skinned

2 shallots, finely chopped

2 garlic cloves, finely chopped

10 g/$\frac{1}{4}$ oz cracked black pepper

sea salt

Suggested wine: Chardonnay San Valentin S. Michel Eppan, 1998, Trentino Alto Adige

Cooking salmon is almost like cooking red meat - it is best done gently and cooked rare.
The temperature of the oil should be no higher than 70°C/175°F. This way you will end up with fish that's pink and perfectly cooked at the centre.

Prepare the cavolo nero sauce. Do not whisk in the final 2 tbsp olive oil until you are ready to serve.
Prepare a bowl of iced water. Blanch the turnips, broccoli, mange-touts, carrots and potatoes in plenty of salted boiling water: the turnips for 2 minutes; the broccoli and mange-touts for 3 minutes each; and the carrots and potatoes for 5 minutes. Refresh in the iced water and drain.
Heat 1 tbsp olive oil in a large pan, add the shallots and garlic, together with the blanched vegetables, and sauté for 2 minutes. Remove the garlic, then set the vegetables aside and keep them warm while you cook the salmon.
Heat the olive oil for cooking the salmon in a deep frying pan until the temperature reaches 70-80°C/175-200°F. Place the salmon in the pan. Cook slowly, over a very low heat, for 10-12 minutes, depending on the size of the portions.
Just before serving, gently reheat the sauce and whisk in 2 tbsp olive oil. Season to taste. Spoon the sauce around 4 warmed serving plates. Slice the salmon pieces in half horizontally and place, cut-side up, on top of the sauce. Sprinkle the cracked black pepper and sea salt over the salmon and garnish with the sautéd vegetables.

Merluzzo mantecato con patate, quaglia arrosto, salsa di broccoli

MASHED COD WITH POTATOES, ROASTED QUAIL AND BROCCOLI SAUCE

4 whole quail, prepared for the oven

100 ml/3¹/₂ fl oz quail jus or chicken jus (see page 17-18)

100 ml/3¹/₂ fl oz broccoli sauce (see page 20)

500 ml/18 fl oz court-bouillon (see page 16)

1 large waxy potato

150 g/5¹/₂ oz cod fillet, skinned

150 g/5¹/₂ oz undyed smoked haddock fillet, skinned

500 ml/18 fl oz milk

100 ml/3¹/₂ fl oz olive oil

2 garlic cloves

salt and white pepper

70 g/2¹/₂ oz butter

1 small radicchio Trevigiano, finely sliced into julienne strips

10 g/¹/₄ oz Parma ham, finely sliced into julienne strips

Suggested wine: Chardonnay Gaia Rey A. Gaja, 1996, Piemonte

Cod, especially salt cod or *baccola* is very popular in Italy, particularly in Veneto and Fruili Venezia Giulia. Here I have used fresh cod and matched it with quail and radicchio to make an unusual but memorable dish.

Ask your butcher to joint the quails and remove the breast meat from the bone. Reserve the carcass if you are making the quail jus.
Make the broccoli sauce but do not whisk in the olive oil until just before serving. Have ready the court-bouillon.
Cook the potato in its skin in boiling water until tender, for 10-15 minutes, then peel it and push it through a sieve or potato ricer into a bowl. While the potato is cooking poach the cod fillet in the court-bouillon and the haddock in the milk for 3 minutes each.
Warm the olive oil in a pan, then add the whole, peeled cloves of garlic and fry gently for a couple of minutes - do not let them burn. Remove the garlic and set aside the oil.
Remove the cod and haddock from their poaching liquids and place them in a food processor, reserving the milk. Process on a low setting, gradually adding the crushed potato. Add the garlic-infused olive oil and mix again until thoroughly combined. Season and allow to rest in the fridge for 1 hour.

Leaving the mixture to rest allows the flavours to mingle properly.

Heat half the butter in a pan and sauté the radicchio and ham for about 30 seconds. Set aside.
Melt the remaining butter in another pan, season the quail breasts and legs and cook for 3 minutes, skin-side down for the breasts, leaving the breast pink. Remove the breasts, cover and set aside. Cook the legs for 2 more minutes.
Warm the cod, haddock and potato mixture in a pan, together with 2 tbsp poaching milk. Warm the broccoli sauce in another pan, then whisk in 1 tbsp olive oil to finish. Season to taste. Gently reheat the quail or chicken jus. Slice each quail breast in half.
Use 2 teaspoons to shape the potato and fish mixture carefully into 12 quenelles or oval shapes. Pour a little broccoli sauce into the centre of 4 warmed serving plates and place 3 quenelles on top of each.
Arrange the sautéed radicchio and Parma ham between these. Place 2 quail legs per person over the radicchio and top with the sliced quail breast. Serve with the warmed jus.

⑧

Filetto di San Pietro arrosto, verza saltata all 'aceto, salsa di zucca

ROASTED FILLET OF JOHN DORY WITH SAVOY CABBAGE, AND PUMPKIN SAUCE

300 ml/10 fl oz
pumpkin sauce
(see page 91)

2 tbsp olive oil

4 John Dory
fillets, each
about 150-175
g/5½-6 oz, skin
on

salt and white
pepper

200 g/7 oz savoy
cabbage, trimmed
and sliced into
julienne strips

2 tbsp red wine
vinegar

200 g/7 oz
pumpkin flesh,
sliced into half-
moon shapes

15 g/½ oz sugar

20 g/¾ oz
butter, diced

Suggested wine:
Batar,
'Quarciabella',
1996, Toscana

John Dory is an extremely versatile fish, full of flavour, and one of my favourites to cook with. The pumpkin sauce in this recipe is based on the pumpkin soup recipe given earlier in this book - simply make it with less stock for a slightly thicker consistency. I've added a few drops of vinegar to the cabbage to counterbalance the sweetness of the pumpkin.

Prepare the pumpkin sauce according to the recipe. Don't whisk in the olive oil until you are ready to serve.
Heat 1 tbsp olive oil in a sauté pan, season the John Dory fillets and cook, skin-side down, for 6 minutes. Turn over and cook the other side for 2 minutes.
Prepare a bowl of iced water. Blanch the sliced cabbage in plenty of boiling salted water. Refresh in iced water and drain. Heat 1 tbsp olive oil in a pan and sauté the sliced cabbage for 2 minutes. Add the wine vinegar and cook for another 30 seconds. Remove from the heat.
Blanch the pumpkin slices in plenty of boiling salted water for 2-3 minutes, then drain. Place the pumpkin in a heavy-based dry frying pan and sprinkle over the sugar. Cook the pumpkin and sugar over a very low heat until the sugar starts to turn golden brown, shaking the pan to stop the sugar from burning. Add the butter and continue to cook for about 2 minutes until the pumpkin has caramelized. Gently heat the pumpkin sauce, whisk in the olive oil and season to taste.
Spoon the sauce over 4 warmed serving plates, then place the sautéed cabbage leaves over the sauce. Top with the John Dory fillets and garnish with the caramelized pumpkin.

9

Filetto di San Pietro alle bietole, ceci saltati

FILLET OF JOHN DORY WITH SWISS CHARD AND SAUTEED CHICKPEAS

50 g/1³/₄ oz tomato concassée

375 ml/13 fl oz olive oil

375 g/13 oz Swiss chard

1 garlic clove, crushed

2 eggs, beaten

150 g/5¹/₂ oz breadcrumbs

4 John Dory fillets, about 175 g/6 oz each, skin on

salt and white pepper

THE CHICKPEA SAUCE
150 g/5¹/₂ oz dried chickpeas

1 tbsp olive oil

¹/₂ onion, roughly chopped

1 carrot, roughly chopped

1 celery stalk, roughly chopped

3 garlic cloves, crushed

1 bouquet garni (see page 188)

pinch of salt

about 500 ml/18 fl oz vegetable stock (see page 17) or water

Suggested wine: Chardonnay 'Coret' Schreckbichl Colterenzio, 1996, Trentino Alto Adige

Swiss chard and chickpeas are a popular combination in Tuscany. As with all my vegetable sauces, if you thin it down with a little more stock you can serve this chickpea sauce as a soup.

Start the chickpea sauce the night before. Soak the chickpeas overnight in water, then drain them.

Heat 1 tbsp olive oil in a large heavy-bottomed casserole, then add the onion, carrot, celery and garlic and sauté for 3 minutes. Add the chickpeas, bouquet garni, a pinch of salt and enough water or vegetable stock to cover. Lower the heat and simmer very gently, uncovered, for 40 minutes or until the chickpeas are tender.

Drain the chickpeas and vegetables, reserving the cooking liquid. Remove the vegetables, garlic and bouquet garni from the chickpeas and discard. Set one half of the chickpeas to one side for the garnish. Purée the other half in a blender or food processor with about two-thirds of the cooking liquid, then pass through a chinois or fine-meshed sieve into a clean pan.

In a separate pan warm the whole chickpeas with 1 tbsp of the cooking liquid, then add the tomato concassée and 1 tbsp olive oil. Remove from the heat and keep warm.

Take 250 g/9 oz of the Swiss chard and cut the green leaves into triangle shapes and the white central stalk into fine julienne strips. Heat 1 tbsp olive oil in a pan, add the crushed garlic and sauté the julienne strips for 1 minute. Add the green leaves and cook for another 2-3 minutes. Remove from the heat, remove the garlic, and keep warm.

Cut the white central stalks of the remaining Swiss chard into 20 diamond shapes, each about 4 cm/1½ in long. Blanch these in plenty of boiling salted water, then drain. Dip each diamond into the beaten egg, then into the breadcrumbs. Repeat so that they are thoroughly coated. Heat 300 ml/½ pint olive oil in a deep pan until the temperature reaches 150°C/300°F and fry the diamonds until crisp. Remove to a plate lined with kitchen paper.

Heat 2 tbsp olive oil in a frying pan, season the John Dory and sauté, skin-side down, for 4-6 minutes. Turn the fish over and sauté for another 2 minutes.

Gently heat the chickpea sauce, then whisk in the olive oil to finish. Spoon the sauce over 4 warmed flat serving plates and put the sautéed Swiss chard over the sauce. Top with the John Dory, then garnish with the whole chickpeas and tomatoes, and the Swiss chard diamonds.

Ragu di scampi e animelle con patate e carciofi

RAGOUT OF LANGOUSTINES AND SWEETBREADS WITH POTATOES AND ARTICHOKES

400 g/14 oz calves' sweetbreads (3 pieces per person)

12 new potatoes

6 tbsp olive oil

115 g/4 oz butter

4 garlic cloves, crushed

2 thyme sprigs

1 rosemary sprig

lemon juice

12 baby artichokes

300 ml/½ pint vegetable stock (see page 17)

3 tbsp dry white wine

100 ml/3½ fl oz shellfish stock (see page 16)

75 ml/2½ fl oz veal jus (see pages 17-18)

salt and white pepper

12 langoustines or tiger prawns, shelled and deveined

Suggested wine: Pinot Bianco Jermann 1997 Friuli Venezia Giulia

Sweetbreads are a great delicacy in Italy and their mild and delicate flavour is well worth sampling. Only the sweetbreads from lambs or calves are used in cooking. You may need to order them in advance from your butcher. For a vegetarian dish omit the sweetbreads and replace the veal jus with vegetable stock.

Prepare the sweetbreads by soaking them in water for 3-4 hours. Blanch them in salted boiling water for 6-7 minutes, then drain and leave to cool. Peel off the membranes using a small sharp knife, and trim away any nerves or veins.
Preheat the oven to 180°C/350°F/gas mark 4.
Peel the new potatoes and 'turn' them by shaping into six-sided cylinders with a sharp knife. Blanch them in plenty of boiling salted water for 5 minutes; remove them when the water comes back to the boil. Meanwhile warm 2 tbsp olive oil with 50 g/1¾ oz butter in a roasting pan. Add 2 garlic cloves, 1 thyme sprig and the rosemary. Drain the potatoes, place them in the roasting pan and sauté for 2-3 minutes. Roast in the oven for 15 minutes until nicely browned.
Prepare a bowl of acidulated water (water with lemon juice). Peel off the tough outer leaves from the artichokes until you reach the tender heart, then cut off the top third and scoop out the choke. Slice off a small amount of the green stalk at the bottom. Put the artichoke hearts in the water as you prepare them to stop them from turning brown.
Heat 1 tbsp olive oil in a large casserole and add 2 garlic cloves and 1 thyme sprig. After 30 seconds, add the artichokes. Heat the stock in separate pan. Add the wine to the artichokes and once it has evaporated, add the hot stock. Cover the casserole and cook for 10 minutes until the artichokes are tender.
Heat 2 tbsp oil in a pan and sauté the sweetbreads until crisp and well coloured - about 5 minutes. Add 35 g/1¼ oz butter, reduce the heat to very low and leave to cook slowly for another 5 minutes.
Heat the shellfish stock until reduced by half, then add the veal jus and reduce again by half. Season to taste, then whisk in the remaining butter to finish.
Heat 1 tbsp olive oil in a pan and sauté the langoustines for 4 minutes. Arrange 3 sweetbreads, 3 langoustines, 3 roast potatoes and 3 baby artichokes on each of 4 warmed serving plates. Spoon the sauce over the top.

❶❶

Scampi arrosto con lenticchi, fagioli e orzi perlato

ROASTED LANGOUSTINES WITH A RAGOUT OF PULSES

200 g/7 oz
lentils

200 g/7 oz pearl
barley

200 g/7 oz
cannellini beans

4 tbsp olive oil

2 carrots,
roughly chopped

2 leeks, roughly
choppped

2 onions, roughly
chopped

2 celery stalks,
roughly chopped

8 garlic cloves,
crushed

3 bouquets garnis
(see page 188)

1 l/1³/₄ pints
vegetable stock
(see page 17) or
water

150 ml/¹/₄ pint
olive oil

3 rosemary sprigs

100 g/3¹/₂ oz
tomatoes
concassées (2
tomatoes)

salt and white
pepper

20 langoustines
or tiger prawns,
shelled and
deveined

Suggested wine:
Pinot Bianco
Venica e Venica,
1997, Friuli
Venezia Giulia

Langoustines and pulses make the perfect combination for prince and pauper. The langoustine, with its sweet, delicate taste, is the king of shellfish, while pulses are a storecupboard basic. I also love the contrast in texture between the smooth, fleshy shellfish and the rougher-textured lentils. You will need to start soaking the pulses the night before.

In three different bowls soak the lentils, barley and beans overnight in plenty of water.
Drain the pulses. Heat 1 tbsp olive oil in each of 3 different sauté pans and add one-third of the carrots, leeks, onions and celery to each pan, together with 2 garlic cloves and 1 bouquet garni in each. Cook for 3 minutes until everything starts to colour, then add the pulses, each type in a separate pan. Pour in enough vegetable stock or water to cover, then simmer until tender. The cannellini will need 25 minutes, the barley 20 minutes and the lentils 15 minutes.
Remove the vegetables, garlic and bouquets garnis from the pans and discard, then combine all the pulses in 1 pan.
Warm the remaining 150 ml/¹/₄ pint olive oil in a pan, add the rosemary sprigs and 2 garlic cloves and leave to infuse over a low heat for 5 minutes. Remove the rosemary sprigs and garlic. Toss the pulses with the rosemary-flavoured oil, then stir in the tomato concassée and seasoning. Cover and keep warm.
Heat 1 tbsp olive oil in a sauté pan, season the langoustines and sauté for 4 minutes.
Divide the pulses among 4 warmed serving plates and top with the langoustines.

Astice al vapore con polenta bianca e funghi di bosco

STEAMED LOBSTER WITH WHITE POLENTA AND WILD MUSHROOMS

4 live lobsters, about 350 g/ 12 oz each

4 red peppers

salt and white pepper

6 tbsp olive oil

300 g/10¹/₂ oz fine-grained white polenta

about 2 l/3¹/₂ pints court-bouillon (see page 16)

200 g/7 oz wild mushrooms, such as porcini, cleaned

1 garlic clove, crushed

100 ml/3¹/₂ fl oz shellfish stock (see page 16)

Suggested wine: Chardonnay Tasca d'Almerita, 1997, Sicilia

Polenta is a staple ingredient all over the north of Italy and usually forms part of a hearty rustic meal. The lobster is quite an extravagant addition but, as with all shellfish, it is the perfect foil to this bland and comforting grain. Use a copper pan if you have one - this helps the polenta to cook evenly. Otherwise use a pan with a heavy base.

To kill the lobsters lay each one stomach downwards on the worksurface, then pierce through the crossmark on the skull with the tip of a large sharp knife. Set aside.
Preheat the oven to 180°C/350°F/gas mark 4. Place the whole peppers on a roasting tray, sprinkle with salt and drizzle over 1 tbsp olive oil. Cook in the oven for 10-15 minutes until soft. Remove from the oven, cover with clingfilm, then place in a sealed plastic container. Once the peppers are cool enough to handle remove the clingfilm, peel them and cut each one into petal-shaped slices, discarding any seeds.
Bring 800 ml/1⅓ pints salted water to the boil in a heavy-based pan - use a copper pan if you have one. Add 3 tbsp olive oil, then gradually add the polenta in a steady stream, whisking all the time. Cook for 40 minutes over a low heat, stirring frequently with a wooden spoon. The polenta is ready when it comes away easily from the sides of the pan. When the polenta is nearly cooked, preheat the oven to 100°C/175°F/gas mark low. In a large pan or stockpot bring the court-bouillon to the boil. Plunge the lobsters in the court-bouillon and cook for 5-6 minutes, depending on size. Remove from the court-bouillon and set aside to cool. Once the lobsters are cool enough to handle, remove the claws and head. Open the claws with kitchen scissors and remove the meat, preferably in 1 piece. Cut the tails in half lengthways and scoop out the meat from the shell, trying to keep the pieces whole. Place the lobster meat in a roasting pan and cover with a clean dampened kitchen towel. Place in the oven to warm.
Heat 1 tbsp olive oil in a sauté pan. Add the mushrooms and sauté with the garlic for 4-5 minutes.
Heat the shellfish stock until reduced by half, then whisk in 1 tbsp olive oil. Season to taste. Remove the garlic.
Spoon the polenta over 4 warmed serving dishes, place the lobster meat on top, arrange the mushrooms around the lobster and pour the sauce over the mushrooms. Garnish with the roasted pepper petals.

Cappesante e patate, melanzane secche, salsa leggera all'aglio

---

GRILLED SCALLOP AND POTATO WITH OVEN-DRIED AUBERGINE AND GARLIC
MAYONNAISE

salt

1/2 aubergine,
peeled and finely
sliced into 12

3 tomatoes confit
(see page 188),
each cut into
4 'petals'

1 tbsp
vinaigrette (see
page 189)

3 medium potatoes
(King Edward or
Italian Spunta),
peeled and each
sliced into 4

2 tbsp olive oil

12 scallops,
cleaned and roes
removed

20 g/3/4 oz frisée
lettuce

THE MAYONNAISE
6 garlic cloves,
unpeeled

10 g/1/4 oz rock
salt

1 thyme sprig

150 ml/1/4 pint
olive oil, plus
1 tbsp

2 egg yolks

1/4 tsp English
mustard

few drops of
lemon juice

salt and white
pepper

Suggested wine:
Pinot Grigio
'Dissimis' Vie di
Romans, 1997,
Friuli Venezia
Giulia

This recipe makes a delicious light lunch for summer. It could also be served as a starter.

To make the mayonnaise, first prepare a garlic purée. Preheat the oven to 180°C/350°F/gas mark 4. Place the garlic cloves in the centre of a large square piece of kitchen foil, sprinkle over the rock salt and thyme and drizzle over 1 tbsp olive oil. Close up the foil to make a sealed package and cook in the oven for 10-15 minutes. Leave to cook slightly, then slip each clove of garlic out of its skin into a chinois or fine-meshed sieve and press them through the sieve into a bowl.
Add the egg yolks, a pinch of salt and the mustard to the garlic purée and whisk until combined. Now add the remaining 150ml/1/4 pint olive oil, one drop at a time, whisking after each drop. After you have added a few drops of oil the mixture should start to thicken. You can now add the oil in a steady trickle. It's very important to add the oil slowly at the beginning - if you don't, the mixture may curdle. Once you have a thick, glossy mayonnaise add the lemon juice and check for seasoning.
Reduce the oven temperature to very low. Sprinkle some salt over the base of a non-stick pan, then add the aubergine slices and cook in the oven for about 1 hour, until they have dried out. Turn them over after 30 minutes. Remove from the oven, set aside and keep warm.
While the aubergines are drying, make the tomatoes confit and prepare the vinaigrette.
Trim the potato slices by cutting them into neat circles with a 5 cm/2 in round pastry cutter. Blanch the circles in boiling salted water for 5-6 minutes. Drain and toss with 1 tbsp olive oil. Heat a ridged cast-iron grillpan and cook the potatoes for 5 minutes on each side.
Season each scallop with salt and drizzle over 1 tbsp oil. Cook in the grillpan for 3 minutes on 1 side. Set aside and keep warm.
Place 3 aubergine slices on each warmed plate, and on top of these place the potatoes and then the scallops. Toss the frisée with the vinaigrette and place a little at the centre of each serving. Garnish with the tomato petals and the garlic mayonnaise.

Meat, poultry

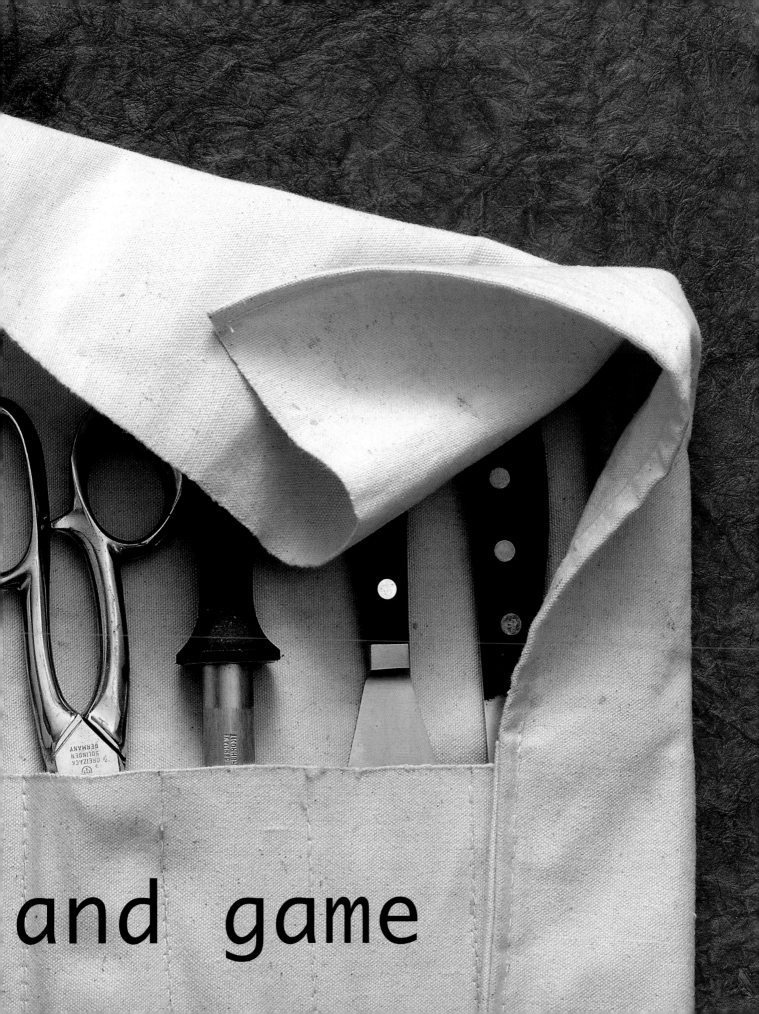

and game

❶

Filetto di vitello al prosciutto, patate arrosto, pomodori, funghi e zucchine

ROASTED FILLET OF VEAL WITH PARMA HAM, ROASTED POTATOES, TOMATOES, MUSHROOMS AND COURGETTES

50 g/1¾ oz caul fat

4 veal fillets, about 175 g/6 oz each

8 slices Parma ham

20 new potatoes

6 tbsp olive oil

100 g/3½ oz butter

1 rosemary sprig

3 garlic cloves, crushed

3 courgettes

85 g/3 oz shiitake mushrooms, cleaned and cut into 1 x 1 cm/½ x ½ in cubes

85 g/3 oz black pitted olives, finely diced

100 g/3½ oz tomatoes concassées (2 tomatoes)

150 ml/¼ pint veal jus (see page 17-18), or concentrated beef stock

salt and white pepper

Suggested wine: Barbaresco Vanotu Pelissero, 1997, Piemonte

Caul fat is the fine, lacy membrane that lines the stomach of a pig. It's often used as a basting layer for roasting delicate meats and it melts into nothing after cooking, leaving behind a golden-brown crust. The sweet-salty flavour of the Parma ham is wonderful with the veal, which is rendered beautifully tender by the protective wrapping of caul fat.

First, prepare the caul fat by soaking it in lukewarm water for about 1 hour, until softened.

Trim the veal fillets of any fat, then wrap a piece of Parma ham round each fillet. Cut the softened caul fat into squares 10 x 10 cm/4 x 4 in and wrap these tightly around the veal and Parma ham to seal the meat completely.

Preheat the oven to 200°C/400°F/gas mark 6.

Trim the new potatoes by 'turning' them into oval shapes with a sharp knife. Blanch them in plenty of boiling salted water, removing them when the water returns to the boil, then drain and pat dry. Heat 2 tbsp olive oil with 50 g/1¾ oz butter in a roasting pan, add the potatoes and sauté in the hot fat for 5 minutes. Roast in the oven for 15-20 minutes. After 5 minutes add the rosemary and garlic.

While the potatoes are cooking heat 1 tbsp olive oil with 50 g/1¾ oz butter in an ovenproof casserole and add the veal parcels. Cook for 4-5 minutes until browned all over. Transfer the pan to the oven and cook for 10 minutes. The veal is ready when the centre of the meat is 58°C/150°F when tested with a meat thermometer - it should still be pink at the centre. Remove from the oven and leave to rest for 10 minutes.

Meanwhile, using a small parisienne scooper, cut the unpeeled courgettes into small spheres. Alternatively, peel the courgettes and finely dice the peel into pieces 1 x 1 cm/½ x ½ in.

Heat 1 tbsp olive oil in a sauté pan. Add the courgette pieces and sauté for 1 minute, then add the mushrooms. Cook for 3 minutes. Remove from the heat and add the olives and tomato concassée.

Heat the veal jus in a small pan until reduced by half, then whisk in 2 tbsp olive oil. Season to taste. Pour the jus over the courgette, mushroom, olive and tomato mixture.

Slice each veal parcel into 3 pieces. Divide the vegetable mixture among 4 warmed serving plates and top with the veal. Garnish with the roast potatoes.

Carre di vitello al forno con salsa ai porcini

OVEN-BAKED LOIN OF VEAL WITH WILD MUSHROOM SAUCE

2 kg/4¹/₂ lb veal loin, bone in (4 cutlets)

2 tbsp olive oil

125 g/4¹/₂ oz butter

200 g/7 oz spring onions, trimmed and finely sliced into julienne strips

1 garlic clove, crushed

1 thyme sprig

1 rosemary sprig

150 g/5¹/₂ oz wild mushrooms, such as porcini, cleaned and finely sliced into julienne strips

4 garlic cloves, crushed

2 garlic cloves, crushed

50 ml/2 fl oz vegetable stock (see page 17)

3 tbsp veal jus (see pages 17-18), or concentrated beef stock

leaves from 3 flat-leaf parsley sprigs, finely chopped

salt and white pepper

Suggested wine: Ornellaia Tenute dell' Ornellaia, 1996, Toscana

This is my version of scallopini e funghi - veal with mushrooms - a very well-known dish in Italy. If you don't feel like cooking a roast, ask your butcher to cut the veal into cutlets instead. Simply cook them under a grill or in a ridged griddle pan and serve with the mushroom sauce. If you use dried mushrooms, reserve the soaking water for making the sauce.

Preheat the oven to 180-200°C/350-400°F/gas mark 4-5. Trim the veal of any fat and trim away any meat or fat from around the emerging bones. Tie the veal loin with kitchen string so that it keeps its shape during cooking. Season the meat with salt and pepper.

Heat 1 tbsp olive oil with 50 g/1¾ oz butter in a large sauté pan and add the meat to seal it. Cook until the meat is browned all over. Remove the meat from the pan and set aside. Wipe the pan, then melt 50g/1¾ oz butter in the pan and sauté the spring onions until they start to colour. Place the browned veal on top of the spring onions. Add 4 cloves of garlic, thyme and rosemary and pour in the vegetable stock. Place in the oven and cook for 40 minutes until the temperature at the centre of the meat is 58°C/150°F when measured with a meat thermometer.

Remove the veal from the pan, cover with kitchen foil and set aside to rest for 15-20 minutes.

Heat 1 tbsp olive oil in another pan and sauté the mushrooms with 2 crushed garlic cloves for 3-4 minutes.

Make the sauce in the pan in which you cooked the veal. Discard the garlic, rosemary and thyme, but leave in the spring onions. Skim the fat from the surface, then add the sautéed mushrooms, the veal jus and the parsley. Heat gently and whisk in the remaining butter to finish. Season to taste.

Cut the veal into 4 cutlets and serve with the sauce on the side.

❸

Costoletta di vitello alla milanese

VEAL CUTLET IN BREADCRUMBS

4 veal cutlets,
about 175 g/6 oz
each, bone in

salt and white
pepper

2 eggs, beaten

400 g/7 oz fresh
breadcrumbs

200 g/7 oz butter

150 g/6 oz
broccoli, cut
into florets

1 tbsp
olive oil

2 lemons
(optional)

Suggested wine:
Donna Lisa Leone
de Castris 1995
Riserva Salice
Salentino

This is a classic Milanese dish. Make the breadcrumbs from the inside of a fresh white sandwich loaf, discarding the crust. Don't season the veal with salt, as this encourages the juices to come out of the meat and spoils the breadcrumb crust.

Trim the cutlets of any fat and season the meat with pepper. Dip the cutlets into the beaten egg and then into the breadcrumbs. Repeat so that they are well coated.
Heat the butter over a very gentle heat. When the butter starts to sizzle add 2 cutlets and cook on one side for 7-8 minutes. Keep the heat low so that a nice golden crust is able to form without the butter burning. Turn the cutlets over and cook for another 3-4 minutes. Remove from the pan to a plate lined with kitchen paper, and cover to keep warm. Wipe out the pan and add the remaining butter, then cook the remaining cutlets in the same way.
Prepare a bowl of iced water. Blanch the broccoli florets in plenty of boiling salted water, then refresh in the iced water and drain. Heat 1 tbsp olive oil in a sauté pan, season the broccoli and sauté for 2 minutes.
In Milan this dish is served with lemons, but I omit them because I find that the juice makes the breadcrumbs go soggy. However, if you like the flavour of lemons and want to serve them, cut the lemons in half and wrap each half in a square of muslin - this prevents seeds and pith escaping when you squeeze them. Secure the ends with a piece of string. Serve the cutlets with the broccoli and with 1 lemon half per person.

❹

Coscia d'agnello da latte con salsa ai carciofi e patate arrosto

LEG OF LAMB WITH ARTICHOKE SAUCE AND ROAST POTATOES

1 leg of lamb, about 1.25 kg/ 2³/₄ lb

200 ml/¹/₃ pint artichoke sauce (see page 19)

1 head of garlic, 3 cloves finely chopped and the rest crushed

salt and white pepper

5 thyme sprigs

6 rosemary sprigs

5 tbsp olive oil

150 g/5¹/₂ oz butter

1 carrot, diced

1 celery stalk, diced

1 onion, diced

3 tbsp white wine

vegetable stock (see page 17), for basting

25-30 new potatoes

100 ml/3¹/₂ fl oz lamb jus (see pages 17-18)

Suggested wine: Brunello di Montalcino Caparzo, 1990, Toscana

In Liguria lamb is often cooked with artichokes in a fricassée. In this recipe I have made use of this match of flavours in a slightly different way, by pairing a simple roast with a delicious artichoke sauce.

Ask your butcher to bone the leg of lamb partially, removing just the top part of the bone and butterflying the meat. Leave the thigh bone and meat in place. Keep the bone for making the sauce.
Prepare the artichoke sauce, but do not whisk in the olive oil until ready to serve.
Preheat the oven to 180-200°C/350-400°F/gas mark 4-5.
Lie the lamb flat on the worksurface, and spread out the butterflied meat. Sprinkle over the chopped garlic, seasoning, and 3 sprigs each of thyme and rosemary. Roll the meat up to enclose the herbs and seasoning and tie with kitchen string. Season the leg all over.
Heat 1 tbsp olive oil and 50 g/1¾ oz butter in a roasting pan, add the lamb and cook until browned all over. Add the diced carrot, celery and onion, together with 2 crushed garlic cloves and 2 sprigs each of thyme and rosemary. Add the lamb bone to the pan and rest the leg on top. Sprinkle over the white wine and place in the oven. Roast for 40 minutes. After about 10 minutes add 1 glass vegetable stock or water to the pan and baste if the meat appears dry.
Peel and shape the potatoes into ovals by 'turning' them with a sharp knife (see page 189). Blanch them in boiling salted water, removing them when the water returns to the boil, and drain thoroughly. Heat 2 tbsp olive oil in another roasting pan, add the potatoes and turn them to coat in the fat. Sauté in the fat for 5 minutes. Place in the oven and cook for another 5 minutes until golden brown. Add 1 sprig of rosemary, 2 crushed garlic cloves and 50 g/1¾ oz butter, then return to the oven for another 5 minutes.
When the lamb is ready - it should be pink on the inside and the temperature at the centre should be 60°C/160°F - remove it from the oven, transfer to a warmed serving dish, cover with kitchen foil and leave to rest for 10-15 minutes.
Pour the lamb jus into the roasting pan with the bone, add 300 ml/½ pint water and bring to a simmer, stirring to scrape up all the vegetables and bits from the bottom. Heat to reduce by half. Skim and strain the sauce into a clean pan and bring to the boil. Remove from the heat and whisk in the remaining butter to finish. Warm up the artichoke sauce and whisk in 2 tbsp olive oil to finish.
Slice the lamb and serve with the artichoke sauce, roast potatoes and lamb jus.

Rognone di vitello alla griglia, salsa di aglio e prezzemolo

GRILLED KIDNEYS WITH SAUTEED SPINACH, PARSLEY AND GARLIC SAUCE

2 calves'
kidneys, about
350 g/12 oz each,
cleaned of fat

salt and
white pepper

2 tbsp olive oil,
plus 1 tbsp for
brushing

20 g/1 oz rock
salt

1 thyme sprig

7 garlic cloves,
unpeeled

12 slices
pancetta

400 g/14 oz
spinach

25 g/1 oz butter

150 ml/5¹/₂ fl oz
veal jus (see
pages 17-18) or
concentrated beef
stock

leaves from 2
parsley sprigs,
chopped

Suggested wine:
Barolo Bricco
Rocca Vigna Big
Roccadei Manzoni,
1995, Piemonte

Offal, particularly liver and kidneys, is used commonly in Italian cooking. Tender kidneys from very young animals are a particular speciality, as they have a very delicate flavour.

Remove the membranes from the kidneys, then slice each kidney in half. Using a pair of scissors snip out any fatty strands. Sprinkle the kidneys with salt and leave to soak in water for 1 hour. If the kidneys are very young, and have no odour, you won't need to salt and soak them. Rinse thoroughly, then leave under cold running water for about 30 minutes.

Meanwhile make the garlic purée. Preheat the oven to 180°C/350°F/gas mark 4. Place 1 tbsp olive oil, the rock salt, thyme and garlic cloves on a square of kitchen foil. Close up the foil to make a sealed parcel and bake in the oven for 10-12 minutes.

Cut each slice of pancetta into 3 pieces and place on a baking tray. Cover the tray with another one of the same size to keep the pancetta flat, place in the oven and cook for 5 minutes until crispy.

Heat a ridged cast-iron griddle pan. Drain the kidneys, brush them all over with 1 tbsp olive oil and season with salt and pepper. Grill them for 4-5 minutes on each side, until browned but still pink in the middle.

Clean and wash the spinach, then drain it thoroughly. Heat the butter in a pan and sauté the spinach with a pinch of salt for 4 minutes. Heat the veal jus in a pan until reduced by two-thirds. Press the baked garlic through a chinois or fine-meshed sieve into the reduced veal jus. Add the chopped parsley leaves and whisk in 1 tbsp olive oil to finish.

Place the spinach in the centre of 4 warmed serving plates. Arrange the grilled kidneys over the spinach, pour the sauce around and garnish with the crispy pancetta.

6

Animelle alle nocciole, tortino di vegetali

SWEETBREADS IN A HAZELNUT SAUCE WITH VEGETABLE TART

700 g/1 lb 10 oz calves' sweetbreads

2 tbsp olive oil, plus extra for brushing

70 g/3½ oz butter

1 small aubergine, very finely sliced

1 large courgette, very finely sliced

2 plum tomatoes, very finely sliced

salt and white pepper

50 g/1¾ oz hazelnuts

150 ml/¼ pint veal jus (see pages 17-18), or concentrated beef stock

Suggested wine: Poliziano 'Asione' Vino Nobile di Montepulciano, 1996, Toscana

This masterpiece was created by Gualtiero Marchesi. The vegetable tarts are also good served with roast meats or on their own as a light starter.

Prepare the sweetbreads by soaking them in water for 3-4 hours. Blanch them in salted boiling water for 6-7 minutes, then drain and leave to cool. Peel off the membranes using a small sharp knife, and trim away any nerves or veins. Cut the sweetbreads into 12 even-sized portions. Preheat the oven to 180°C/350°F/gas mark 4.

Heat 1 tbsp olive oil in a roasting pan and brown the sweetbreads all over, then roast in the oven for 4-5 minutes. Add 35 g/1¼ oz butter, reduce the heat to 150°C/300°F/gas mark 2 and return to the oven for another 3 minutes. Leave the oven on for cooking the vegetable tarts.

To make the tarts, brush the aubergine, courgette and plum tomato slices with olive oil. Cut out 4 circles of greaseproof paper 10-12 cm/4-5 in in diameter, place them on a baking sheet or tray and arrange the slices on top so they overlap in neat circles. Sprinkle with salt and drizzle over 1 tbsp olive oil. Cook in the oven for 6-7 minutes.

Place the hazelnuts in a roasting pan and roast in the oven for 3-4 minutes, until brown but not burnt. Roughly chop the nuts in a food processor or with a sharp knife. Heat the veal jus in a pan until reduced by two-thirds, then add half of the chopped hazelnuts. Whisk in the remaining butter to finish. Season to taste.

Carefully slide the vegetable tarts off the greaseproof paper on to 4 warmed serving plates. Top with the sweetbreads, spoon the sauce over, and garnish with the remaining chopped hazelnuts.

Pollanca bollita e farcita al tartufo nero, mostarda di frutta e salsa verde

POACHED HEN WITH BLACK TRUFFLES, FRUIT MUSTARD AND GREEN SAUCE

2 hens, approximately 1.25 kg/2³/₄ lb each, boned and jointed

25 g/1 oz black truffle, finely sliced

100 ml/3¹/₂ fl oz madeira

¹/₂ shallot, finely chopped

450 ml/16 fl oz double cream

2 carrots

¹/₂ celeriac bulb

1.5 l/2³/₄ pints chicken stock (see page 17)

8 new potatoes

FOR THE SALSA VERDE leaves from small bunch flat-leaf parsley

115 g/4 oz giardiniera

4 anchovy fillets

10 capers

1 boiled egg, shelled

3 slices of baguette soaked in white wine vinegar

300 ml/¹/₂ pint olive oil

salt and white pepper

Suggested wine: A Kronte Boccadi Gabbia, 1994, Marche

The classic dish of Bollito Misto comes from the area around Verona. Here is a variation on this simple recipe - the truffles transform it into a delightful dish for a dinner party or special occasion.

Mostarda di frutta (candied fruit in a mustard-flavoured syrup) can be found in most Italian delis and supermarkets. You can also buy jars of *giardiniera* (vegetables pickled in vinegar) in most large supermarkets. A hen is the female egg-laying bird or *gallina*, and is usually sold in butchers' shops as boiling fowl. For this recipe you should try to buy a young good-quality hen. Best of all would be a Bresse hen, which you may need to order in advance.

Ask your butcher to joint and bone the boiling fowl, and reserve the carcass if you are making your own stock.

Make the salsa verde by blending all the ingredients together in a food processor. Season to taste with salt and pepper.

Take the 4 hen breasts and, using the fingers of one hand, ease the skin away from the meat to make a pocket. Place the truffle slices under the skin of the breasts, reserving about one-eighth for the stuffing.

Cut the boned legs in half and set aside the top parts of the legs. Carefully remove the skin from the bottom part of the legs and cut the meat into pieces. Blend in a food processor until very fine. Finely chop the reserved truffle, add this to the chopped meat with the madeira, the shallot and the cream, and pulse until combined. Use this mixture to stuff the cavity inside the top part of the leg left by the bone. Secure the opening with string. These stuffed legs are called roulades.

Slice the carrots and celeriac into rectangular pieces approx 4 x ¹/₂ cm/ 1¹/₂ x ¹/₄ in. Bring the stock to the boil in a pan, then add the carrots, celeriac, potatoes and roulades.

Wrap the roulades in clingfilm to help them keep their shape while they are cooking.

After 4-5 minutes add the breasts and reduce the heat to a gentle simmer. After about 8-10 minutes remove the breasts and set aside. After 12-15 minutes remove the pan from the heat.

Unwrap the roulades and slice into rounds. Serve 1 breast and 1 sliced roulade per person. Divide the vegetables among 4 plates and pour a little broth around each serving, or place the breasts and legs on one large serving plate with the broth poured over.

Serve with fruit mustard and the salsa verde.

Petto di pollo farcito al limone, timballo di vegetali

CHICKEN BREAST STUFFED WITH LEMON, WITH VEGETABLE TIMBALE

100 g/3½ oz caul fat (see page 128)

3 unwaxed lemons, plus juice of 1

300 ml/½ pint olive oil

35 g/1¼ oz sugar

85 g/3oz salt, plus extra salt and white pepper

4 chicken supremes, each about 175 g/6 oz, bone in, skin on

1 tbsp olive oil

100 g/3½ oz butter

1 thyme sprig

1 rosemary sprig

1 garlic clove, crushed

3 tbsp chicken jus (see pages 17-18)

250 g/9 oz spinach

THE TIMBALES
4 plum tomatoes confit (see page 188)

1 large potato, peeled and very finely sliced

4 tbsp olive oil

2 aubergines, finely sliced

salt and white pepper

2 courgettes, very finely sliced

Suggested wine: Gravello Librandi, 1994, Calabria

In Italy chicken is often stuffed with lemon before being roasted. Here, I have created a variation on this theme by stuffing individual chicken supremes with slices of fragrant lemon confit, and serving them with a delicious lemony sauce.

Soak the caul fat in lukewarm water until soft - about 1 hour.
Cut the lemons into slices ½ cm/¼ in thick, or as thinly as you can, and place in a thick-based pan with the olive oil, sugar and salt. Leave to cook over a very low heat, without covering the pan, for 1 hour.
Make the vegetable timbales. First prepare the tomatoes confit, leaving the oven on low for warming the timbales. Cook the potato slices in boiling salted water for 8-9 minutes until tender, then drain.
Heat 2 tbsp olive oil in a pan, add the aubergines, season and sauté for 3-4 minutes, turning them once. Remove from the pan to a plate lined with kitchen paper. Add 2 tbsp olive oil to the pan, add the courgettes, season, and sauté for 3-4 minutes, turning them frequently - you may need to do this in batches. Remove to another plate lined with kitchen paper.
Take 4 x 5 cm/2½ in timbale moulds and place on a non-stick baking tray. Make a layer of potato slices in the base of each, then top with a layer of aubergine, then courgette. Follow with one more layer of aubergine and another of courgette. Finish with a layer of tomato confit. Place in the oven to keep warm.
Take the lemon slices out of the liquid with a slotted spoon and remove any seeds. Carefully push the lemon slices under the skin of the chicken breasts. Remove the caul fat from the water and drain. Using kitchen scissors cut it into slices large enough to wrap up each chicken breast - about 30 x 25 cm/12 x 10 in. Wrap the breasts in the fat so that all the meat is covered. Heat 1 tbsp olive oil and 50 g/1¾ oz butter in a pan and add the chicken. Cook for 3-4 minutes on each side. Add 20 g/¾ oz of the butter, and the thyme, rosemary and garlic. Cook for another 5-6 minutes. Remove the chicken from the pan and leave to rest for 5-10 minutes. Tip away the fat from the pan, add the lemon juice to the pan to deglaze it and heat until evaporated. Add the chicken jus and heat until reduced by two-thirds. Strain into a clean pan.
Heat 20 g/¾ oz butter in a pan, add the spinach, season with salt and sauté for 3-4 minutes, then divide among 4 warmed serving plates. Slice each chicken breast diagonally into 3 pieces and place on top of the spinach. Unmould the timbales and place 1 on each plate. Gently heat the sauce then whisk in the remaining butter. Spoon the sauce around the chicken or serve separately.

❾

Piccione in salsa di ciliege e amarone, spinaci saltati

PIGEON WITH RED CHERRY AND AMARONE SAUCE, AND SAUTEED SPINACH

4 whole pigeons, prepared for the oven

salt and white pepper

2 tbsp olive oil

85 g/3 oz butter

2 garlic cloves, crushed

1 thyme sprig

1 tbsp Amarone wine, or other good quality red wine

150 ml/¼ pint pigeon jus or chicken jus (see pages 17-18)

25 sweet red cherries, pitted

250 g/9 oz spinach

Suggested wine: Amarone Mithas Corte S'Alda, 1990, Veneto

One evening I was at my mother's house sharing a bottle of wine with my friend, Stefano dal Pozzo also a chef. We started to feel hungry, so looked in my mother's fridge to see what she had. As luck would have it, we found two pigeons, killed that morning. As it was June there were cherries everywhere - so, using these ingredients, we created this dish.

Ask your butcher to joint the pigeon and bone the breasts and legs, reserving the bones if you are making the jus.

Season the breasts and legs. Heat the olive oil in a pan, add the legs and the breasts, skin-side down first, and sauté for 2-3 minutes on each side - the breast meat should stay pink at the centre. After about 3 minutes add 25 g/1 oz butter, and the garlic and thyme. Remove the breasts, cover and set aside to rest. Cook the legs for another 5 minutes until the skin is crispy. Remove the legs from the pan, cover and set aside to rest for 5 minutes.

Discard the fat from the pan and return the pan to the heat, then pour in the Amarone wine to deglaze. Heat until the wine has evaporated, then add the jus and reduce again by two-thirds. Pass the sauce through a chinois or fine-meshed sieve into a clean pan and whisk in 25 g/1 oz butter to finish. Season to taste. Add half the cherries to the sauce. Set aside and keep warm.

Heat the remaining butter in a pan, add the spinach and a pinch of salt and sauté for 4-5 minutes.

Divide the spinach among 4 warmed serving plates. Slice each pigeon breast diagonally into 3 pieces and place on top of the spinach. Add 2 legs to each serving and pour the sauce around. Garnish with the remaining cherries.

Petto d'anatra alla menta, indivia belga saltata

BREAST OF DUCK WITH MINT AND SAUTEED ENDIVE

1 tbsp olive oil

4 duck breasts,
each about
175 g/7 oz,
skin on

salt and white
pepper

100 g/3½ oz
butter

2 small rosemary
sprigs

1 thyme sprig

4 garlic cloves,
crushed

2 heads of
Belgian endive
(chicory)

juice of 1 lemon

150 ml/¼ pint
duck jus (see
pages 17-18)

10 mint leaves,
finely sliced
into julienne
strips

THE TIMBALES
3 tbsp olive oil

2 small
aubergines, very
finely sliced

salt and white
pepper

2 courgettes,
very finely
sliced

2 tomatoes, very
finely sliced

Suggested wine:
Duca Enrico
Salaparuta, 1995,
Sicilia

Duck with mint is a classic combination.
I've taken this idea as a starting point, but
given it a modern note by lightly sautéing
the duck breasts with rosemary and garlic, and
adding endive as a contrasting flavour.
Summer is the perfect time to try this dish,
as fresh mint is abundant. At other times of
year you could substitute finely sliced black
olives for the mint.

To make the vegetable timbales, preheat the oven to 120°C/225°F/gas mark
¾. Heat 1 tbsp olive oil in a large sauté pan, add the aubergine slices,
season and sauté for 3-4 minutes, turning once. Remove from the pan to a
plate lined with kitchen paper. Heat another tbsp olive oil in the pan,
add the courgette, season and sauté for 3-4 minutes, turning frequently.
Remove to another plate lined with kitchen paper. Season the tomatoes
with salt and drizzle over 1 tbsp olive oil. Take 4 x 8 cm/3 in timbale
moulds and place on a non-stick baking tray. Layer the vegetables inside
the moulds starting with the aubergine, then the courgettes and
tomatoes. Repeat to make a total of 6 layers. Cook in the oven for 10
minutes until tender. When ready to serve invert each mould on to the
plate so that the aubergine layer is uppermost.
Heat 1 tbsp olive oil in a pan, season the duck breasts and sauté, skin-
side down first, for 4-5 minutes on each side - the meat should still be
pink inside. After 5 minutes add 40 g/1¾ oz of the butter, the rosemary,
thyme and garlic. Remove the breasts from the pan, cover and set aside
to rest for 10 minutes.
Prepare a bowl of iced water. Trim the endive, remove the bitter core
and separate the leaves. Blanch the leaves in boiling salted water and
lemon juice (the lemon juice stops the endive from turning brown).
Refresh in the iced water and drain thoroughly. Heat 20 g/¾ oz butter in
a pan, add the endive and a pinch of salt and sauté for 3-4 minutes.
Heat the duck jus in a small pan until reduced by two-thirds, then whisk
in the remaining butter. Season to taste.
Divide the endive leaves among 4 warmed serving plates, slice the duck
breasts diagonally and place on top. Stir the sliced mint leaves into
the sauce and pour around the duck, or serve the sauce separately. Serve
with the vegetable timbales.

⏸ Germano reale al miele e aceto balsamico

ROAST MALLARD WITH HONEY AND BALSAMIC VINEGAR

100 g/3/¹/₂ oz new potatoes

4 mallard or duck, prepared for the oven

salt and white pepper

4 tbsp olive oil

5 garlic cloves, crushed

2 thyme sprigs

50 g/1³/₄ oz butter

2 rosemary sprigs

1 tbsp balsamic vinegar

2 tbsp honey

175 ml/6 fl oz duck or chicken jus (see page 17-18)

100 g/3/¹/₂ oz mange-touts

100 g/3/¹/₂ oz courgettes

100 g/3/¹/₂ oz broccoli

100 g/3/¹/₂ oz spring onions

100 g/3/¹/₂ oz carrots

Suggested wine: Amarone, Pergole Vece Lessalette, 1995, Veneto

This is a delicious way of roasting a bird: the honey and balsamic vinegar add a subtle sweetness to the dish that really brings out the gamey flavour of the mallard. If mallard is not available, use duck instead.

Preheat the oven to 200C/400F/gas mark 6.
Shape the potatoes by 'turning' them with a sharp knife (see page 189), then blanch them in boiling salted water.
Meanwhile season the outside of the mallards or ducks with salt. Drain the potatoes, then place in a roasting pan with 1 tbsp olive oil, 2 garlic cloves and the thyme sprigs.
Cook in the oven for about 10 minutes until golden.
Heat 2 tbsp olive oil in a roasting pan, add the mallards or ducks and brown on all sides for 5 minutes. Transfer the birds to the oven and cook for a further 10-15 minutes, depending on size. After about 7 minutes add 25 g/1 oz of the butter, 3 garlic cloves and the rosemary sprigs to the pan.
This cooking time will leave the breast pink and tender; the legs will need another 10 minutes, so remove them and return to the oven separately.
They can be served on the side, or you can keep them to make a confit (see page 188).
Remove the birds from the pan, cover and set aside to rest.
Skim the fat from the roasting pan and return the pan to the heat. Add the balsamic vinegar and honey and heat to reduce the liquid by half. Add the jus and reduce again by two-thirds, then whisk in the remaining butter to finish.
Prepare a bowl of iced water. Trim the vegetables and chop into pieces of approximately the same size. Blanch them in boiling salted water for about 2 minutes, then drain and refresh in the iced water. Heat 1 tbsp olive oil in a pan and sauté the vegetables for 2-3 minutes.
Serve the birds on a large warmed serving dish with the vegetables on one side. Serve the sauce separately.

Pernice al melograno, rape confit, pure di sedano rapa

PARTRIDGE WITH POMEGRANATES, TURNIP CONFIT AND CELERIAC PUREE

4 partridges,
prepared for
the oven, or
4 partridge
breasts, skin on

1 celeriac, 500-
600 g/1 lb 2oz-
1 lb 5 oz, peeled
and diced

2 tbsp olive oil

500 g/1 lb 2 oz
butter, for
poaching the
turnips, plus
85 g/3 oz

salt and white
pepper

5-6 medium
turnips, peeled
and sliced 2 cm/
1 in thick

150 g/5½ oz
pumpkin (¼ of 1
medium pumpkin),
cut into half-
moon shapes
1 cm/½ in thick

35 g/1¼ oz sugar

2 pomegranates

1 tbsp white wine

150 ml/¼ pint
partridge jus or
chicken jus (see
pages 17-18)

50 g/2 oz grated
Parmesan

3 tbsp whipping
cream

Suggested wine:
Serpico I Feudi
di San Gregorio,
1995, Campagla

Roast partridge is a traditional British dish and, like roast pheasant, it is normally served with bread sauce. This is my version, which, I'm happy to say, does without the bread sauce. Partridge are at their best in October or November. Try to buy wild red-legged partridge (*pernice rossa*) rather than farm-reared grey-legged birds, as they have a more delicate flavour. You can buy partridge breasts in the gourmet section of some large supermarkets.

If you are buying a whole partridge, ask your butcher to joint the partridge and bone the breasts. Reserve the carcass if you are making the jus and keep the legs for another recipe.

Cook the diced celeriac in plenty of salted boiling water for 7-10 minutes until tender, then drain and purée in a food processor or blender. Pass the purée through a chinois or fine-meshed sieve on to a square of muslin. Tie into a loose bundle and suspend from a wooden spoon resting over a bowl. Leave to drain for at least 1 hour, or overnight if possible.

Heat 2 tbsp olive oil and 35 g/1¼ oz butter in a pan, season the breasts and cook for 2-3 minutes on each side, skin-side down first, until pink inside. Remove, cover and leave to rest.

Clarify the butter (see page 188), then gently heat it in a pan to about 60°C/160°F. Poach the turnip slices in the butter for 20 minutes, or until tender. Set aside and keep warm.

Blanch the pumpkin slices in plenty of boiling salted water, then drain. Sprinkle the sugar into a heavy-based pan and heat gently until it starts to colour. Add the pumpkin and 35 g/1¾ oz butter and cook over a gentle heat for 3-4 minutes, shaking the pan so that the sugar doesn't burn, until caramelized. Set aside and keep warm.

To make the sauce, quarter the pomegranates. Remove the seeds and place in a bowl. Discard the fat from the pan in which you cooked the partridge breasts. Heat the pan and deglaze with the white wine. Heat until the wine has evaporated. Put the pomegranate seeds in a sieve and gently press them over the pan to extract the juice, then tip the seeds into the pan as well. Add the jus, heat gently to reduce slightly, then whisk in the remaining butter to finish. Strain and season to taste.

Place the celeriac purée in a pan, add the Parmesan and cream and heat gently. Season to taste.

To serve, place the turnip slices on 4 warmed serving plates. Top with 2 partridge breasts per person. Serve with the celeriac purée, caramelized pumpkin and pomegranate sauce.

149

Sella di capriolo con salsa ai mirtilli, ravioli di zucca e castagne

SADDLE OF VENISON WITH BLUEBERRY SAUCE PUMPKIN AND CHESTNUT RAVIOLI

4 portions saddle
of venison,
trimmed and
boned, about
175 g/6 oz each
(boned weight)

salt and white
pepper

2 tbsp olive oil

1 medium potato,
King Edward or
Italian Spunta,
peeled and very
finely sliced
(32-40 slices)

20 g/³/₄ oz black
winter truffle,
sliced into 20
pieces

250 g/9 oz savoy
cabbage, trimmed
and sliced into
julienne strips

150 ml/¹/₄ pint
venison or veal
jus (see pages
17-18)

350 g/12 oz
butter, plus
35 g/ 1oz

140 g/5 oz
blueberries

THE RAVIOLI
85 g/3 oz
pumpkin, skin on

50 g/1³/₄ oz
chestnuts,
skinned and
chopped

20 g/³/₄ oz
grated Parmesan

salt and white
pepper

50 g/1³/₄ oz fresh
pasta dough
(see page 56)

Venison has less fat and cholesterol than any
other meat, so is an excellent choice if you are
trying to eat healthily. If you don't have time
to make the ravioli, serve pumpkin purée as an
accompaniment instead. Buy vaccum-packed chestnuts
for the ravioli filling; they usually come already
peeled and cooked, in packs of 200 g/7 oz.

Ask your butcher to trim and bone the venison and reserve the bones if
you are making the jus.
Preheat the oven to 150°C/300°F/gas mark 2. Wrap the pumpkin in kitchen
foil and cook in the oven on a baking sheet for 30 minutes. Cut the
pumpkin flesh away from the skin and pulse to a purée in a food
processor. Pass through a chinois or fine-meshed sieve on to a square of
muslin. Tie it up into a loose bundle and suspend from the handle of a
wooden spoon over a bowl. Leave to drain for at least 1 hour.
Make the pasta dough, then divide into 4 equal pieces. Pass the dough
through the pasta machine, finishing at the lowest setting, until you
have 4 very thin, almost transparent sheets (see page 56). Transfer to a
lightly floured surface. Make the ravioli as for the duck ravioli (see
page 60), spacing the chestnut-and-pumpkin filling 4 cm/1½ in apart, and
cutting circles with a 4 cm/1½ in round pastry cutter. Set aside on a
tray dusted with semolina flour and cover with a cloth until needed.
Sprinkle the venison fillets with salt and pepper. Heat 1 tbsp olive oil
in a large pan and add the venison. Cook for 8-10 minutes until pink on
the inside and brown all over. The temperature at the centre should read
58°C/150°F on a meat thermometer. Cook longer if you prefer it well
done. Remove from the pan, cover with kitchen foil and leave to rest.
Shape the potato slices into circles with a 4 cm/1½ in round pastry
cutter. Top each circle with a slice of truffle, then with another
potato circle, to make 8 or 10 per person. Clarify the butter (see page
188). Heat the clarified butter in a pan and sauté the potato parcels
for 4-5 minutes, turning carefully, until crisp.
Blanch the savoy cabbage in salted boiling water, then drain. Heat 1
tbsp olive oil in a pan, add the cabbage, sprinkle over some salt and
sauté for 3-4 minutes until tender.
In the same pan as you cooked the venison heat the jus until reduced by
two-thirds. Whisk in 20 g/¾ oz butter and stir in the blueberries.
Cook the ravioli in boiling salted water for 3-4 minutes, then drain and
sauté with the remaining butter for 30 seconds.
Slice the venison. Divide the cabbage among 4 warmed serving plates, and
top with the venison and ravioli. Pour the sauce around and garnish with
the crispy potato and truffles.

Desserts,
pastries
and bread

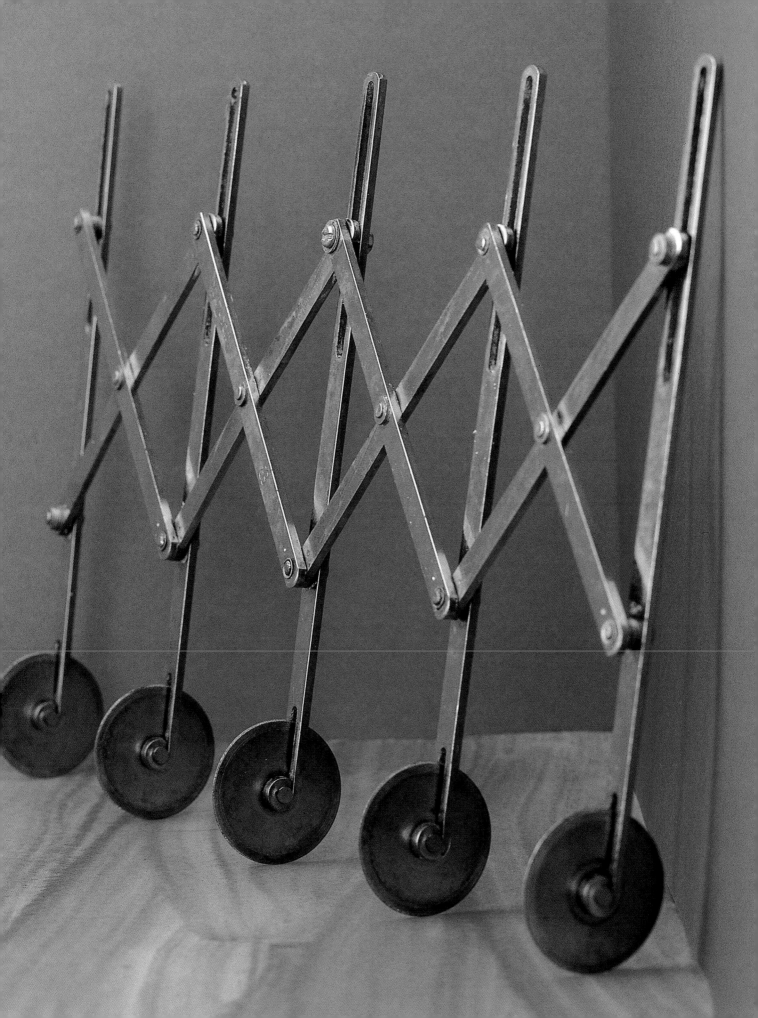

masterclass 5: zabaione al moscato rosa

ZABAIONE WITH MOSCATO ROSA WINE

THE ZABAIONE
8 egg yolks

85 g/3 oz sugar

300 ml/½ pint moscato rosa wine

savoiardi biscuits (see below)

icing sugar

50 g/1¾ oz each strawberries, blackberries, blueberries and raspberries

mint leaves, to garnish

THE SAVOIARDI BISCUITS
Makes 24

4 egg yolks

100 g/3½ oz sugar

60 g/2¼ oz cornflour

60 g/2¼ oz plain flour

3 egg whites

icing sugar, for dusting

Zabaione is probably one of the best-known Italian desserts. It is a supremely simple recipe, with only three key ingredients: eggs, sugar and alcohol. It is not difficult to make, but you must be sure not to let the eggs overheat and you should be prepared to serve it as soon as it is ready. Traditionally it is made with marsala, but this delicate moscato wine adds a pretty pink tinge to the zabaione. You can vary the flavourings - try using champagne, rum or a sweet dessert wine - but remember that it will only taste as good as the wine you use, so choose the best quality you can find. Zabaione ice-cream is an easy variation on this recipe. Simply prepare the zabaione and allow to cool slightly. Fold in 500 ml/18 fl oz whipped cream and pour into moulds or ramekins. If you line the moulds first with pieces of greaseproof paper that are about 5 cm/2 in taller than the moulds, you will achieve a 'tower' effect when you remove the paper from the frozen desserts. At the restaurant we serve zabaione with a langue-de-chat basket filled with red fruits. Here I've left out the basket, serving the zabaione with the fruit and biscuits instead.

1 Beat the egg yolks in a large heatproof or metallic bowl for 30 seconds.

2 Place the sugar and wine in a heavy-based pan and heat gently, stirring, until the sugar has dissolved to make a syrup.

3 Bring the syrup to the boil and pour into the beaten yolks, whisking as you do so.

4 Place the heatproof bowl containing the syrup and eggs over a pan of gently simmering water; the bowl should fit snugly but should not touch the water.

5 Whisk steadily for about 20 minutes over a gentle heat, using a figure of eight motion to incorporate maximum air, until the mixture has risen and doubled in volume. Do not on any account let it boil or the eggs may curdle and you will have to start again with fresh ingredients. It will be ready when you can see the bottom of the bowl as you whisk.

6 Pour the zabaione into 4 large dessert glasses or wine glasses and serve with the savoiardi biscuits dusted with icing sugar and the red fruits decorated with mint leaves.

THE SAVOIARDI BISCUITS

1 Preheat the oven to 200°C/400°F/gas mark 6 and line a baking tray with baking parchment.

2 Whisk the egg yolks with 40g/1½ oz of the sugar in a heatproof bowl set over a pan of simmering water, until they are lukewarm. Remove the bowl from the heat and beat with electric beaters for 10 minutes until pale yellow and doubled in volume.

3 Sieve the cornflour and flour into the egg yolk-and-sugar mixture and fold in gently.

4 Beat the egg whites with the remaining 60g/2¼ oz sugar until stiff peaks form, then carefully fold them into the egg-and-flour mixture, one-third at a time.

5 Spoon the mixture into a piping bag fitted with a small plain nozzle. Pipe 24 short lengths about 4 cm/1½ in long on to the baking parchment. Sprinkle sugar over the top and bake for 10 minutes until just golden.

6 Remove from the oven and place on a wire rack to cool.

❶

Parfait ghiacciato al caffe con salsa mandorle e fichi

ICED COFFEE PARFAIT WITH ALMOND SAUCE AND MARINATED FIGS

500 ml/18 fl oz
double cream

50 g/1¾ oz
coffee beans

7 egg yolks

150 g/5½ oz
sugar

2½ tbsp Tia
Maria

6-8 fresh figs

500 ml/18 fl oz
Cassis

mint leaves, to
garnish

THE ALMOND SAUCE
100 g/3½ oz
marzipan

2 tbsp Amaretto
di Saronno

250 ml/9 fl oz
milk

125 ml/4 fl oz
whipping cream

5 egg yolks,
beaten

Suggested wine:
Passito di
Pantelleria Ben
Rye 'Donna
Fugata', 1998,
Sicilia

This elegant recipe brings together three
flavours that have a very special affinity.
You will need to start making the parfait
the day before, as it needs to freeze overnight.

First make the parfait mixture. Bring 150 ml/¼ pint cream to the boil
with the coffee beans, remove from the heat and leave to cool slightly.
Strain into a bowl and leave to cool completely. Add the remaining cream
and beat with electric beaters until nice and stiff.
Whisk the egg yolks with the sugar in a heatproof bowl set over a pan of
simmering water so that it fits snugly - the base should not touch the
water. When the mixture is lukewarm remove from the heat and whisk for
10-15 minutes until pale and thick. When you draw a spoon through the
mixture the base of the bowl should be visible.
Fold the cream into the egg-yolk mixture, one-third at a time, using a
metal spoon. Finally, gently fold in the Tia Maria to taste - do not
overmix or it may split.
Place 4 x 6-7 cm/2½-3 in ring moulds on a tray lined with greaseproof
paper and pour in the parfait mixture. Place in the freezer and leave
overnight.
Peel the figs, cut them in half and marinate in the Cassis for 2 hours.
To make the sauce, put the marzipan in a microwave-proof bowl and
microwave for 10 seconds on a medium setting to soften it. Add the
Amaretto and work it into the marzipan with a wooden spoon until creamy,
then place in a pan with the milk and cream. Heat gently, stirring,
until the mixture comes to the boil, then remove from the heat.
Gently beat the 5 egg yolks together in a heatproof bowl. Add the yolks
to the marzipan mixture and stir to combine. Place the bowl over a pan
of just-simmering water and heat gently until the mixture thickens -
about 5-7 minutes - stirring constantly. Do not allow the mixture to
boil or it may curdle.
Remove from the heat and leave to cool.
Remove the parfait from the freezer and leave for 2-3 minutes to soften
slightly before unmoulding. Spoon the sauce around 4 serving plates, top
with the parfait and decorate with 3 or 4 half figs per person. Garnish
with the mint leaves.

❷

Terrina di cioccolato con salsa di arance e mandarini cinesi

CHOCOLATE TERRINE WITH ORANGE AND KUMQUAT SAUCE

THE SPONGE
4 eggs, separated

85 g/3oz sugar

25 g/1 oz plain
flour

25 g/1 oz cocoa
powder

THE SYRUP
35 g/1¼ oz sugar

2 tbsp rum

THE FILLING
3 egg yolks, plus
1 whole egg

40 g/1½ oz sugar

200 g/7 oz dark
chocolate (70-75%
cocoa solids),
roughly chopped

125 ml/4 fl oz
double cream

THE SAUCE
100 g/3½ oz
kumquats

60 g/2 oz sugar

100 ml/3½ fl oz
fresh orange
juice

TO SERVE
8 oranges, peeled
and segmented

peel of 2
oranges, blanched
3 times and
finely sliced

15 g/½ oz
pistachios

8 raspberries

mint leaves

Suggested wine:
Vigna La Miccia,
De Bartoli,
Sicilia

This is a classic Sicilian recipe, and one of
my favourite desserts. I love the combination
of dark, smooth chocolate with the tang of orange.
In Sicily they would use blood oranges - as you
could, too, if they're in season.

Preheat the oven to 220°C/425°F/gas mark 7.
Rest a large heatproof bowl over a pan of simmering water so that it
fits snugly without touching the water. Whisk the egg yolks for the
sponge with 20 g/¾ oz sugar in the bowl until warm - about 5 minutes.
Remove the bowl from the heat and beat the mixture until it falls from
the whisk in a thick ribbon. Beat the whites with the remaining sugar to
form stiff peaks.
Sieve the flour and cocoa powder into the yolk mixture, then gently fold
in the egg white with a metal spoon, one-third at a time. Pour into a 20
x 15 cm/8 x 6 in swiss-roll tray lined with baking parchment to no more
than 1 cm/½ in thick. Bake for 10-15 minutes, until golden.
Remove from the oven and leave to cool slightly. Invert the sponge on to
a wire rack and remove the baking parchment. Take a 1 kg/2 lb loaf tin
and draw round the base on to a piece of baking parchment. Cut this out,
then use it as a template to cut out 4 rectangular layers of sponge.
To make the syrup, place 2 tbsp water in a heavy-based pan and heat
gently, stirring in the sugar until dissolved. Bring to the boil then
remove immediately from the heat. Set aside to cool completely, then
stir in the rum.
To make the filling, whisk the yolks and whole egg with the sugar in a
large heatproof bowl over a pan of barely simmering water until they are
lukewarm. Remove from the heat and beat for 10-15 minutes until pale and
creamy. Melt the chocolate in another bain-marie then add it to the egg
mixture, whisking gently from the bottom of the bowl upwards. Whip the
cream until thickened, then fold into the chocolate mixture.
Line the terrine with clingfilm, leaving an overhang of 13 cm/5 in all
round. Place 1 sponge layer in the base. Spoon over a little rum syrup,
then spread over one-third of the chocolate filling. Top with another
layer of sponge and repeat until you have 4 layers of sponge and 3 of
chocolate. Cover with clingfilm and freeze overnight.
For the sauce, blanch the kumquats for 7 minutes. Drain and refresh in
iced water, then dice. Place in a pan with the sugar and 75 ml/2½ fl oz
water. Cook for 10-15 minutes until tender, then pass through a chinois
or fine-meshed sieve into a pan. Add the orange juice and bring back to
the boil until reduced by two-thirds. Pass through the sieve once more.
Unmould the terrine and cut into slices. Serve with the sauce, and
garnish with the orange segments, peel, chopped pistachios, raspberries
and mint leaves. Dust with icing sugar.

❸

Datteri farciti con mousse di cioccolato bianco, insalata di mandarini

STUFFED DATES WITH WHITE CHOCOLATE MOUSSE AND SATSUMA SALAD

THE WHITE
CHOCOLATE MOUSSE
1 gelatine leaf

250 ml/9 fl oz
whipping cream

125 g/4½ oz
good-quality
white chocolate,
chopped

cocoa powder, for
dusting

THE SATSUMA SALAD
4 satsumas

8 mint leaves,
finely chopped

1 tbsp fresh
orange juice

12 fresh dates

Suggested wine:
Marsala
Garibaldi,
'Pellegrino',
Sicilia

This simple dessert is a lovely balance of light and rich flavours. The satsumas cut through the richness of the chocolate and act as a refreshing palate cleanser.
Try to use gelatine leaves rather than gelatine powder, as they dissolve more evenly. If you can't find leaves half a teaspoon gelatine powder is the equivalent of one leaf.

Soak the gelatine leaf in cold water for 10 minutes. Strain the leaf and place it in a small pan over a low heat until melted. Set aside.
Bring 125 ml/4 fl oz of the whipping cream to boil in a pan. Remove from the heat and add the chocolate, stirring until melted. Stir in the gelatine (scrape it from the saucepan with a spatula if necessary) and set aside to cool.
When it has cooled, whip the remaining cream until thick but not too stiff. Carefully fold the cream into the chocolate mixture, starting with 1 tbsp and gradually folding in the rest. Chill for about 2 hours.
To make the salad, divide the satsuma into segments, removing all the pith. Toss the satsuma segments with the chopped mint and orange juice.
Wash, peel and halve the dates. Arrange 6 date halves on each plate.
Spoon the chilled cream into a piping bag fitted with a fine nozzle and pipe the mousse over the dates. Dust with cocoa powder. Arrange the satsuma segments and mint around the dates.

4

Torta al cioccolato

CHOCOLATE TART

THE SWEET PASTRY
100 g/3½ oz butter, diced

100 g/3½ oz icing sugar

2 eggs, beaten

250 g/9 oz plain flour

pinch of salt

THE FILLING
600 g/1 lb 5 oz dark bitter chocolate (70-75% cocoa solids), roughly chopped

10 eggs

100 g/3½ oz sugar

400 g/14 oz butter, melted

Suggested wine:
Marsala Doc Vergine 'Pellegrino' 1996 Sicilia

This is the perfect dessert for chocolate lovers. Eat it on its own, or serve it with crème anglaise flavoured with rum.
Make sure the butter for the pastry is chilled and the eggs are at room temperature.

To make the pastry, put the diced butter in the bowl of a food mixer and sieve the icing sugar over. Using the paddle attachment mix for about 5 minutes until smooth. Gradually add the eggs, making sure they don't curdle, and mix for another 5 minutes. Sieve in the flour and salt, a little at a time, and mix until you have a crumbly dough. Shape into a ball, wrap tightly in clingfilm and leave to rest overnight in the fridge or for 3-4 hours.
Preheat the oven to 200°C/400°F/gas mark 6.
Roll out the pastry on a lightly floured surface to a thickness of ½ cm/¼ in. Use the pastry to line a 20 cm/8 in tart tin with a removable base, leaving a 2 cm/1 in overhang to allow for shrinkage.
Chill the pastry for 20 minutes.
Line the pastry with baking parchment, scatter over baking beans or pearl barley, place on a baking sheet and bake blind for 20-25 minutes until golden. Take out of the oven, remove the paper and beans, and trim the edges with a sharp knife. Reduce the heat to 150°C/300°F/gas mark 2.
To make the filling, put the chocolate in a heatproof bowl over a pan of barely simmering water, making sure the base does not touch the water. Leave to melt, then remove the bowl from the heat.
Whisk the eggs and sugar in a large bowl until stiff. Add the melted butter to the chocolate, then fold carefully into the egg and sugar mixture with a metal spoon, one-third at a time.
Place the pastry case on the oven rack, pour the chocolate filling in and bake for 10-15 minutes.
Allow to cool slightly before serving.

Tiramisù

TIRAMISU

THE COFFEE SAUCE
5 egg yolks

175 ml/6 fl oz whipping cream

175 ml/6 fl oz milk

50 g/1³/₄ oz sugar

4 tbsp strong espresso coffee (made)

1 tsp instant coffee

THE BASKETS
200 g/7 oz icing sugar

85 g/3 oz plain flour

5 egg whites

50 g/1³/₄ oz melted butter

THE MASCARPONE MIX
6 eggs, separated

150 g/5¹/₅ oz sugar

300 ml/10 fl oz double cream

500 g/1 lb 2 oz mascarpone cheese

TO SERVE
8 savoiardi biscuits soaked in 125 ml/4 fl oz strong espresso coffee (made)

10 g/¹/₄ oz cocoa powder

8 chocolate sticks

Suggested wine: Vin Santo di Carmignano, Capezzania, 1992, Toscana

This well-known Italian dessert originated in the Veneto region. When I came to work at the Halkin I decided that I wanted to make my tiramisu look a little different by serving it in a langue-de-chat basket - and I'm flattered to see that my idea has been taken up by many other London restaurants. The original recipe does not contain cream, but I have added some to make a more luxurious version.

Beat the egg yolks in a heatproof bowl. Bring the cream, milk, sugar, espresso and instant coffee to the boil in a pan. Once the mixture is boiling pour it over the beaten egg yolks and stir with a plastic spatula to combine. Return to the pan over a low heat and cook for a few minutes, stirring, until the mixture has thickened enough to coat the back of a spoon - the temperature should be 70°C/100°F. Pass through a chinois or fine-meshed sieve into a clean bowl, cover and leave to cool. To make the baskets, you will need 4 miniature pudding basins or plastic tumblers for moulding the basket shape. Place the icing sugar, flour and egg whites in a food mixer with paddle attachment and process at a low speed for 10 minutes. Pour in the melted butter and beat to combine. Preheat the oven to 180°C/350°F/gas mark 4. Line 2 baking trays with baking parchment. Place 1 ladleful of the mixture on to the centre of the paper on each tray and spread out to make a 20 cm/8 in circle (if you prefer, draw a circle first on the paper as a guide). Cook in the oven for 5-6 minutes until golden. Remove from the oven and immediately ease the circles off the baking parchment with a spatula. Place over the base of the upturned pudding basins or tumblers and mould around to make a basket shape, folding it in pleats where necessary. Leave to cool before unmoulding. Repeat to make 4 baskets.

To make the mascarpone cream, whisk the egg yolks and the sugar in a heatproof bowl over a pan of simmering water, remove from the heat and beat until pale, creamy and doubled in volume. Whisk the egg whites until they form stiff peaks. Whisk the cream until thick. Gradually add the mascarpone cheese to the beaten yolk, folding it carefully with a metal spoon and working from the bottom of the bowl to the top. Fold in the cream, then gently fold in the egg white, one-third at a time. Refrigerate for 2 hours.

Spoon the coffee sauce over the base of each serving plate, then place a basket on top. Spoon 2 tbsp mascarpone mix into the basket then place 2 soaked savoiardi biscuits on top. Top with 2 more tbsp mascarpone, dust with cocoa powder and serve with 2 chocolate sticks.

6

Cannoli alla siciliana

SICILIAN-STYLE STUFFED SWEET PASTA

1 l/1³/₄ pints vegetable oil

1 pineapple, skinned

100 g/3¹/₂ oz sugar

10 each raspberries and blackberries

4 mint leaves

icing sugar

THE PASTA DOUGH
250 g/9 oz plain flour

35 g/1¹/₄ oz sugar

10 g/¹/₄ oz salt

1 egg yolk

100 ml/3¹/₂ fl oz red wine

1 tsp olive oil

THE FILLING
200 g/7 oz ricotta

20 g/³/₄ oz chopped pistachios

20 g/³/₄ oz candied mixed peel, chopped

20 g/³/₄ oz dark chocolate (70-75% cocoa solids), chopped

20 g/³/₄ oz glacé cherries, finely chopped

2 tbsp whipping cream

Suggested wine:
Moscato Passito di Pantelleria Martingana 'Salvatore Murana' 1996, Sicilia

These sweet pasta shapes are sold in almost every pâtisserie in Sicily. In this recipe I've made a more substantial dessert by adding pineapple, but you can eat them on their own at any time of day as a snack.

Start to make the pasta dough the day before. You can buy cannoli moulds from good cookshops. They come in different sizes; here, I have made 4 large cannoli.

To make the dough, sieve the flour, sugar and salt on to a worksurface and make a well in the middle. Whisk the egg yolk with the wine, then pour into the well. Drizzle the oil round the edge. Using your fingers gradually draw the flour into the liquid until you start to form a smooth dough - you may not need to use all the flour. Shape the dough into a ball, wrap in clingfilm and leave to rest in the fridge overnight. Knead the dough the next day, then shape into a ball. Divide the dough into 4 pieces and cover 3 with clingfilm. Flatten the dough slightly then pass it through the pasta machine following the method on page 56 and stopping at around setting number 2, until you have a thin sheet of dough.

Place the sheet on a lightly floured surface and cut it into a rectangle, approximately 10 x 10 cm/4 x 4 in, or large enough to fit round a large cannoli mould. Wrap the rectangle round the mould until the edges meet. Press them together to make a cylinder. Repeat until you have covered all 4 moulds. If you have any pastry left over, keep it in the fridge covered in clingfilm for up to 4 days. You can use it to make sweet, fried tagliatelle, or more cannoli.

Heat the vegetable oil in a heavy-based deep frying pan until it reaches 170-180°C/325-350°F, and deep-fry the cannoli, still on their moulds, until golden. Remove with a slotted spoon to a plate lined with kitchen paper. To make the filling, pass the ricotta cheese through a sieve into a bowl. Mix in the other ingredients, then spoon into a piping bag fitted with a small nozzle.

Slip the cannoli off their moulds and pipe the filling inside.

Cut the pineapple in half. Finely slice one half into rings and roughly chop the other half. Place the chopped pineapple in a food processor and pulse to a purée. Pass through a chinois or fine-meshed sieve.

Mix the sugar with 100 ml/3½ fl oz water and bring to the boil in a small heavy-based pan. Remove from the heat, allow to cool slightly, then stir into the pineapple purée. Arrange the pineapple rings on each serving plate and spoon over the pineapple sauce. Top with the filled cannoli and garnish with the raspberries, blackberries and mint leaves. Dust with icing sugar.

❼

Amaretto creme brûlée con tegole alle mandorle

AMARETTO CREME BRULEE WITH ALMOND TUILES

12 egg yolks

2¹/₂ tbsp Amaretto di Saronno

1 l/1³/₄ pints whipping cream

150 g/5¹/₂ oz sugar

1 vanilla pod

demerara sugar, for sprinkling

mint leaves, to garnish

Almond tuiles, to serve (page 182)

Suggested wine: Malvasia delle Lipari 'Colosi' 1997 Sicilia

Everyone loves crème brûlée. This delicately flavoured Amaretto brûlée makes an interesting change.

Preheat the oven to 150°C/300°F/gas mark 2.
Whisk the egg yolks with the Amaretto in a large heatproof bowl. Put the cream, sugar and vanilla pod in a pan and heat, stirring steadily, until you reach a low boil. Remove from the heat and add the cream mixture to the egg yolks, whisking it in gently as you pour.
Put the kettle on to boil and pour the mixture into 4 x 8 cm/3 in ramekins in a roasting pan. Place on the oven shelf and pour in enough hot (not boiling) water to come halfway up the sides. Bake for 1-1½ hours or until just set. The surface should feel firm, but not solid, when you press it with your fingers. Leave to cool slightly then refrigerate while you make the tuiles.
Preheat the oven to 180°C/350°F/gas mark 4.
Make the tuiles by following the recipe on page 182.
Preheat the grill to high. Sprinkle the sugar over the top of the crème brûlées and place under the grill until the sugar has caramelized.
Decorate with mint and serve with the tuiles.

❽

Millefoglie di lamponi con salsa vaniglia e coulis di lamponi

RASPBERRY MILLEFEUILLE WITH CREME ANGLAISE AND RASPBERRY COULIS

400 g/14 oz puff pastry (see page 22)

125 ml/4 fl oz crème anglaise, to serve

500 g/1 lb 2 oz raspberries

juice of $\frac{1}{2}$ lemon

50 g/1$\frac{3}{4}$ oz sugar

butter, for greasing

THE CREME PATISSIERE

3 egg yolks

85 g/3 oz sugar

40 g/1$\frac{1}{2}$ oz flour

250 ml/9 fl oz milk

1 vanilla pod

250 ml/90 fl oz whipping cream

Suggested wine: Vin Santo Avignonesi, 1989, Toscana

Millefeuille is probably one of the oldest and most fashionable desserts of all. If you prefer, you can substitute the raspberries with strawberries. You should make this dessert at the last minute as leaving it in the fridge will make the pastry go soggy.

Preheat the oven to 220°C/425°F/gas mark 7 and lightly grease a large baking sheet. Roll out the puff pastry on a lightly floured surface to make a large rectangle 30 x 20 cm/12 x 8 in.
Cut into 12 5 x 10 cm/2 x 4 in strips and lift each one carefully on to the baking sheet. Bake in the oven for 15 minutes.
To make the crème pâtissière, whisk the egg yolks with 85g/3oz sugar until the mixture is thick and creamy. Sift in the flour and stir until you have a smooth paste. Place the milk in a pan, split the vanilla pod, add it to the milk and then bring to the boil.
When the milk is boiling remove it from the heat and take out the vanilla pod. Pour the milk into the egg yolk mixture in a steady stream, whisking as you pour. Return to a heavy-based pan and bring to a simmer over a gentle heat, stirring constantly with a wooden spoon. Keeping the heat very low, cook for another 2 minutes, stirring, then strain into a heatproof bowl, cover with clingfilm and leave to cool.
Prepare the crème anglaise while the crème pâtissière is cooling.
Whip the cream until thickened, then stir it, one-third at a time, into the cooled crème pâtissière.
Blend 100 g/3$\frac{1}{2}$ oz of the raspberries with the lemon juice and 40 g/1$\frac{1}{2}$ oz of the sugar, then pass the purée through a chinois or fine-meshed sieve to make a coulis.
Remove the pastries from the oven and lift on to a large worksurface or flat board with a spatula or palette knife. Take 4 pastry rectangles and spread them with one half of the cream mixture. Top with half of the remaining raspberries. Repeat with another 4 rectangles, using the rest of the raspberries and the remaining cream mixture. Place these on top of the first 4, leaving a layer of cream and raspberries exposed.
Take the remaining 4 pastry rectangles and sprinkle them with the remaining sugar. Heat the grill to medium-high, then place the rectangles under the grill until the sugar has melted and caramelized - watch them carefully so that the sugar does not burn. Place these rectangles on top of the layered pastries to make a small tower.
Serve with the raspberry coulis and crème anglaise, spooning them around the pastries.

Pere bollite al pepe nero con parmigiano

POACHED PEARS WITH BLACK PEPPER AND PARMESAN

4 Comice pears

10 g/¼ oz
freshly ground
black pepper

juice of 1 lemon

10 g/¼ oz sugar

¼ cinnamon stick

250 g/9 oz
Parmesan, cut
into chunks

whole peppercorns,
to garnish

Suggested wine:
Torcolato
'Maculan' 1997
Vicenza

It's very common in Italy to eat pears with
Parmesan cheese at the end of a meal.
The poached pears in this recipe add a note of
sweetness, while the black pepper brings out the
flavour of the Parmesan.

Peel the pears, leaving the stalk intact, then core them by scooping out
the base with a parisienne scooper or melon baller. Do not cut them
open.
Place the pears in a large pan with the pepper, lemon juice, sugar and
cinnamon. Add enough water just to cover. Cook over a very low heat
until the pears are tender - about 10-15 minutes.
Remove the pan from the heat and allow the pears to cool in the liquid.
When the pears are cool drain them, reserving the syrup and removing the
cinnamon stick. Using a sharp knife slice the pears neatly from the base
up without cutting through the stalk end.
To serve, fan the pears out on a plate and serve with a little syrup,
the Parmesan and some whole peppercorns to garnish.

Mousse di limone, sciroppo al timo

LEMON MOUSSE WITH THYME SYRUP

40 g/1½ oz
natural yoghurt

50 g/1¾ oz sugar

grated zest of 1
unwaxed lemon

1 tbsp Grand
Marnier

75 ml/2½ fl oz
lemon juice, plus
1 tbsp

1½ gelatine
leaves

200 ml/7 fl oz
whipping cream

THE SYRUP
150 g/5½ oz
sugar

4 thyme sprigs

3 mint leaves,
plus extra to
garnish

juice of 1 lemon

1-2 tsp Grand
Marnier, to taste

Suggested wine:
Picolit Meroi
1996 Colli
Orientali del
Friuli

This combination of citrus fruit with the
clean herb flavours of thyme and mint is
a refreshing way to end a meal. The syrup is
made from an infusion of thyme. If you reduce
the amount of sugar and add a little more
water you can make a lovely chilled drink for
a hot summer's day.

Mix the yoghurt and sugar in a bowl. Add the lemon zest and Grand
Marnier and stir again.
Put the lemon juice in a cup or small bowl. Break up the gelatine leaves
and add to the lemon juice. Set in a pan of barely simmering water until
it has dissolved and become transparent.
Fold the gelatine and lemon juice into the yoghurt mixture.
Whip the cream until thickened but not stiff. Add the cream to the
yoghurt mixture, folding it in gently with a spatula or metal spoon,
one-third at a time.
Divide the mixture among 4 x 8 cm/3 in ramekins and place in the fridge
to set for a couple of hours.
To make the thyme syrup, put 300 ml/10 fl oz water in a heavy-based pan,
add the sugar and heat, stirring, until the sugar has dissolved. Bring
to a gentle simmer. While the syrup is simmering strip the leaves from
the thyme sprigs and add them to the syrup with the mint leaves. Remove
from the heat, add the lemon juice and Grand Marnier to taste, and leave
to cool.
Once the mousse has set, place a shallow soup bowl or serving plate on
top of each ramekin. Invert the ramekin, and carefully unmould the
mousse. Spoon the thyme syrup around the mousse and decorate it with
mint leaves.

To help loosen the mousse, dip each ramekin briefly in a pan of hot water, without
submerging it. If it still does not unmould when inverted, tap the ramekin firmly and
sharply on the base.

Insalata di frutta esotica sciroppo allo zenzero e sorbetto al mango

TROPICAL FRUIT SALAD WITH GINGER SYRUP AND MANGO SORBET

85 g/3 oz each pineapple, mango, kiwi fruit and papaya flesh, diced evenly

20 physalis, leaves removed, halved

40 g/1^{1}/$_{5}$ oz each strawberries, raspberries, blueberries and blackberries

150 ml/^{1}/$_{4}$ pint fresh orange juice (juice of 3-4 oranges)

4 round banana leaves

THE MANGO SORBET
200 ml/^{1}/$_{2}$ pint mango juice

85 g/3 oz sugar

100 g/3^{1}/$_{2}$ oz mango flesh, sliced

juice of 1 lemon

1 tbsp Grand Marnier

100 ml/3^{1}/$_{2}$ fl oz natural yoghurt

THE GINGER SYRUP
200 g/7 oz fresh root ginger

150 g/5^{1}/$_{2}$ oz sugar

Suggested wine: Franciacorta Gran Cuvée Brut 'Bellavista', 1995, Lombardia

This exotic salad is very easy to make and looks wonderful. The ginger syrup gives added 'bite'.
You can easily replace the mango sorbet with a good quality shop-bought ice cream or sorbet.
Banana leaves can be found in Asian grocers and the physalis in Chinese stores.

To make the sorbet, stir the mango juice and sugar together in a heavy-based pan over a gentle heat until the sugar has dissolved. Bring to the boil, then remove immediately from the heat. Put the mango flesh in the heatproof jug of a food processor and pour over the syrup. Pulse to a purée, then pass through a chinois or fine-meshed sieve with the lemon juice into a bowl. Stir in the Grand Marnier and the yoghurt. Transfer to an ice-cream machine, then churn and freeze according to the manufacturer's instructions.
To make the ginger syrup, peel the ginger and grate it. Press the grated ginger through a sieve with the back of a spoon into a heavy-based pan to yield 100 ml/3½ fl oz juice. Add the sugar and 150 ml/¼ pint water to the ginger juice and heat gently, stirring to dissolve the sugar. Bring to the boil, then remove immediately from the heat. Leave to cool. Toss the prepared fruit with the orange juice in a bowl.
Using a 20 cm/8 in paper circle as a guide, trim the banana leaves into rounds. Clean the leaves with a piece of damp kitchen paper. Make a slit at the base of each leaf just past the centre point and at a right-angle to the centre stem, and fold the leaf upwards to make a basket.
Place the baskets on 4 serving plates, then pile the fruit inside and top with the mango sorbet. Pour the ginger syrup over the fruit and decorate with mint leaves.

Gelati e sorbetti

ICE CREAMS AND SORBETS

MASCARPONE ICE CREAM
Makes 1 kg/2 lb 4 oz

500 ml/18 fl oz milk

125 g/4/¹/₂ oz sugar

25 g/1 oz liquid glucose, or
15 g/¹/₂ oz sugar

200 ml/7 fl oz whipping cream

75 g/2³/₄ oz mascarpone

LEMON SORBET, STRAWBERRY SORBET
Makes 1 kg/ 2 lb 4 oz

THE LEMON SORBET
300 g/10¹/₂ oz sugar

500 ml/18 fl oz water

250 ml/9 fl oz freshly squeezed lemon juice (juice of 7-8 lemons)

1 egg white, whisked to soft peaks

THE STRAWBERRY SORBET
150 g/5/¹/₂ oz sugar

500 ml/18 fl oz water

juice of ¹/₂ lemon

300 g/10¹/₂ oz strawberries, puréed and sieved

Everybody likes ice-creams and sorbets - they're the perfect way to round off a meal. If you have an ice-cream maker that can be used in the freezer, they are easy to make at home.

GELATO AL MASCARPONE Mascarpone ice-cream
You can vary this recipe by omitting the mascarpone, or replacing it with 50g/1³/₄ oz finely chopped dark chocolate to make stracciatella. (Italian chocolate-chip ice-cream).

Place the milk, sugar and glucose or sugar together in a heavy-based pan and warm over a low heat until the temperature reaches 85°C/200°F. Keep the temperature steady and cook for 5 minutes, stirring.
Remove from the heat and leave to cool, stirring occasionally to prevent a skin forming.
When the mixture is cool add the cream and mascarpone and stir to combine. Pour into an ice-cream maker and freeze according to the manufacturer's instructions.

SORBETTO AL LIMONE, SORBETTO ALLE FRAGOLE Lemon sorbet, strawberry sorbet
Place the sugar, water and lemon juice or strawberry purée in a heavy-based pan and stir with a wooden spoon over a low heat until the sugar has melted. Remove from the heat and leave to cool, stirring occasionally. For the lemon sorbet, carefully fold the whisked egg white into the cooled mixture. Pour into an ice-cream maker and freeze according to the manufacturer's instructions.

Tegole alle mandorle, ai semi de sesamo e al cocco

ALMOND, SESAME SEED AND COCONUT TUILES

ALMOND TUILES
Makes about 50

200 g/7 oz sugar

125 g/4¹/₂ oz butter, diced, at room temperature

100 ml/3¹/₂ fl oz liquid glucose

100 g/3¹/₂ oz flour

75 g/3¹/₂ oz nibbed almonds

SESAME SEED TUILES
Makes about 50

250 g/9 oz sugar

125 g/4¹/₂ oz sesame seeds

75 g/2³/₄ oz plain flour

100 ml/3¹/₂ fl oz fresh orange juice (juice of 1 orange)

125 g/4¹/₂ oz melted butter

COCONUT TUILES
Makes about 50

150 g/5¹/₂ oz desiccated coconut

175 g/6 oz icing sugar

4 egg whites

125 g/4¹/₂ oz melted butter

In the restaurant we serve these little sweets with coffee at the end of a meal. The tuiles are also good eaten with homemade ice-cream, sorbets, zabaiones and mousses. My recipes make fairly large batches; they may seem like a lot, but it's really not worth making less, and they will keep for a week in an airtight container.

TEGOLE ALLE MANDORLE Almond tuiles
Preheat the oven to 180°C/350°F/gas mark 4.
Place the sugar and butter in the bowl of a food mixer and, using the paddle attachment, cream together until pale. Add the glucose and beat again to combine. Sieve in the flour, a little at a time, beating between each addition. Add the almonds and beat for about 10 minutes. Line a baking sheet with non-stick baking parchment. Use a teaspoon to place little balls of the mixture on the paper, spacing them well apart. Bake in the oven for 6-7 minutes until golden brown. Remove from the oven and, while still hot, use a palette knife to lift each tuile on to a rolling pin or tuile mould to curl them. Leave to cool before removing them carefully.

TEGOLE AI SEMI DI SESAMO Sesame seed tuiles
Preheat the oven to 180°C/350°F/gas mark 4.
Place the sugar, sesame seeds and flour in the bowl of a food mixer and, using the paddle attachment, mix until well blended. Add the orange juice and blend again for 5-6 minutes. Add the melted butter and blend to combine. Line a baking sheet with non-stick baking parchment. Use a teaspoon to place little balls of the mixture on the paper, spacing them well apart. Bake for 6-7 minutes until golden brown. Remove from the oven and shape as above.

TEGOLE AL COCCO Coconut tuiles
Preheat the oven to 180°C/350°F/gas mark 4.
Place the coconut and icing sugar in the bowl of a food mixer and, using the paddle attachment, mix until well blended. Add the egg whites and blend for another 10 minutes. Add the melted butter and blend again to combine. Line a baking sheet with non-stick baking parchment. Use a teaspoon to place little balls of the mixture on the paper, spacing them well apart. Bake for 6-7 minutes until golden brown. Remove from the oven and shape as above.

Piccola pasticceria

PETITS FOURS AND SWEETS

CANDIED ORANGE PEEL
5 oranges, preferably unwaxed

250 g/9 oz sugar

demerara sugar, to serve

LITTLE CHOCOLATES WITH COFFEE GANACHE
Makes about 50-70 chocolates

300 ml/½ pint whipping cream

2 tsp instant coffee granules

900 g/2 lb plain dark chocolate (70% cocoa solids), roughly chopped

1 tbsp Tia Maria

25 g/1 oz cocoa butter

55-70 g/2-2½ oz coffee beans

SCORZE DI ARANCE CANDITE Candied orange peel
If the oranges are waxed, scrub them carefully under warm running water. Using a sharp peeling knife cut the peel from the oranges, leaving the white pith and a thin layer of orange flesh attached. Slice the peel into strips 4-5 cm/1½-2 in long and 1 cm/½ in wide. Prepare a bowl of iced water. Blanch the strips in boiling water three times, removing them from the water as soon as it comes to the boil again and refreshing them in the iced water each time. Place in a heavy-based pan and cover with fresh boiling water. Add the sugar and stir to dissolve. Bring back to a gentle simmer and cover the surface with a circle of baking parchment. Simmer until the peel is transparent - 30-40 minutes. Remove the paper, lift the peel out of the syrup with a slotted spoon and place on a wire rack set above a piece of baking parchment to catch the drips. Leave to dry, then store in a sealed container in the fridge for up to 1 week.
Roll the strips in demerara sugar just before serving.

CIOCCOLATINI AL CAFFE Little chocolates with coffee ganache
Place the cream and coffee granules in a pan and bring slowly to the boil, stirring to dissolve the coffee. Remove from the heat and add 400 g/14 oz of the chocolate, stirring until melted. Add the Tia Maria. Line a shallow plastic container with clingfilm and pour in the chocolate mixture to about 2 cm/¾ in deep. Freeze for 1 hour, or refrigerate overnight, until firm.
Line a baking sheet with non-stick baking parchment.
Melt the remaining chocolate and the cocoa butter in separate bain-maries (see page 188). Once the chocolate has melted stir in the cocoa butter.
Lift the chocolate block from the container and invert it on to a cool surface - marble is ideal. Peel off the clingfilm. Cut into cubes approx 2cm x 2cm/¾ in x ¾ in. Pierce the cubes with a cocktail stick and dip them in the melted chocolate to coat. Place on the lined tray, remove the cocktail stick and top each with a coffee bean. Refrigerate until the chocolate has set, then store in an airtight container in a cool, dry place.

Pane bianco e pane integrale

WHITE BREAD AND BROWN BREAD

Makes 60 rolls

WHITE BREAD
900 g/2 lb strong white flour

20 g/³/₄ oz salt

15 g/¹/₂ oz sugar

25 g/1 oz butter, diced

25 g/1 oz fresh yeast

550 ml/19 fl oz warm water

BROWN BREAD
600 g/1 lb 5 oz strong white flour

200 g/7 oz wholemeal flour

20 g/³/₄ oz salt

15 g/¹/₂ oz sugar

25 g/1 oz butter, diced

25 g/1 oz fresh yeast

550 ml/19 fl oz warm water

You can vary this basic recipe according to taste by adding different herbs, seeds, nuts, olives, onions or tomatoes. Simply add them to the dough with the yeast.

Sieve the flour and salt together in a large mixing bowl. Sieve in the sugar, then add the diced butter and rub in, using the tips of your fingers to make fine crumbs. Dissolve the yeast in 2 tbsp warm water. Make a well and add the yeast liquid and the rest of the warm water, drawing it in with your hands to make a soft dough. Gather it into a ball; it should leave the sides of the bowl clean but should not be sticky or wet. If it is sticky, add a little extra flour; if dry, work in a little extra water.

Turn the dough on to a lightly floured surface and knead thoroughly for 10 minutes. Stretch the dough away from you with the heel of your hand then gather it back into a ball and give it a quarter turn. Continue kneading and turning until the dough is smooth, firm and elastic. Remove the dough to a clean bowl and cover loosely with a cloth. Leave to rest for 30-40 minutes in a warm place.

Knock back the risen dough. Cut the dough into 4 equal strips, then cut each strip into 15 pieces, each weighing approximately 60 g/2¼ oz. Roll each piece out on a floured worksurface and shape into rounds, then place on a greased baking sheet. Cover loosely with clingfilm or a cloth and leave in a warm place for 10-15 minutes.

Preheat the oven to 240°C/475°F/gas mark 9. Place a wide pan at the bottom of the oven and fill with hot water to create steam - this helps the bread to form a crust.

Place the bread in the oven and bake for 20-25 minutes. After about 5 minutes remove the pan of water. To check for doneness, tap the base of the loaf - it should sound hollow.

Glossary and culinary terms

BAIN-MARIE: a waterbath used to cook delicate ingredients such as eggs very slowly over a diffused heat, or for melting chocolate so that it doesn't burn. A double saucepan or boiler is normally used for this; the lower part contains the water and the steam heats the ingredients in the top part. Alternatively, a heatproof bowl can be suspended over a pan of simmering water so that it rests snugly just above the water without touching it. The water should not be allowed to boil in case condensation gets into the ingredients.

BLANCH: fresh vegetables are briefly cooked in water to soften them slightly on the outside while keeping the inside crisp. They are then refreshed in ice-cold water, drained and cooked normally. If you are using lemon or orange zest in a recipe, I recommend you blanch it three times – this will tenderize it without causing it to break up. Place the zest in boiling water, wait 30 seconds until it returns to the boil, then remove and refresh in iced water. Return to the boiling water and repeat.

BRUNOISE: equal amounts of very finely diced vegetables. The resulting mix is used as a flavouring for sauces, and also as a garnish. See mirepoix, below.

BOUQUET GARNI: a bundle of vegetables and aromatic herbs used to flavour a stock or sauce. The ingredients can be tied together with string or enclosed in muslin. A bouquet garni may be made up of carrots, celery, leeks, bay leaves, rosemary and thyme – but this can vary according to what is fresh and available. In the restaurant we use a mixture of celery, carrots, thyme, rosemary, sage and bay leaves. The bouquet garni is removed before serving.

CHINOIS: a fine, conical sieve used for straining sauces, purées or liquid. In the restaurant we use a chinois for all purées and sauces, but this is only essential if you want to achieve a very smooth texture.

CLARIFIED BUTTER: butter that has been melted, then the clear part separated from any impurities on the top and the whey that sinks to the bottom. To clarify butter, melt it gently in a small pan without stirring. Skim off the cloudy top part and decant the clear liquid underneath, making sure that the white residue or whey at the bottom stays in the pan. Clarified butter is used for cooking ingredients at high temperatures – frying, for example - or for long periods of time, such as when making a confit.

CONCASSÉ: a term used to describe a vegetable (usually a tomato), that has been chopped evenly. A tomato prepared in this way is called a tomato concassée: blanch the tomato first in boiling salted water for 2 minutes, then peel, cut into 4, remove the seeds and dice into cubes.

CONFIT: making a confit using goose, duck or pork is one of the oldest ways of preserving meat. The meat is cooked in its own fat, then covered in the same fat to preserve it. It will then keep for several weeks. The word confit is also used to describe slices of vegetables or fruit cooked or dried out for a long time at a very low temperature. These will keep for two or three days if properly stored: if they are dry, in an airtight container, otherwise keep them, in the fridge, covered. To make a confit of tomatoes, preheat the oven to its lowest setting. Blanch the tomatoes as above, then peel them and cut into 4. Remove the seeds, then place in a roasting tray with a few garlic cloves and thyme sprigs. Drizzle over a little olive oil, sprinkle over a little salt and sugar and cook in the oven for 3-4 hours.

COULIS: a liquid purée, used as a sauce or to add flavour to a sauce. To make a tomato coulis, blanch and peel the tomatoes, then purée them in a blender and pass through a chinois or fine-meshed sieve.

DEGLAZE: a small amount of wine, stock or other liquid is added to the hot pan

Glossary and culinary terms

after the main ingredient (usually meat) has been cooked and removed. The cooking juices left in the pan are diluted by the wine or stock and then heated and reduced to make a concentrated base. More liquid can then be added to make a sauce or gravy.

DEVEIN: langoustines and prawns need to have their intestinal sac removed before cooking. This is the long thread or vein that runs along the back of the shellfish – it will be black if the sac is full. Remove by inserting the tip of a sharp knife underneath the vein, then pulling it out carefully.

GARLIC: I always crush peeled garlic cloves with the flat of a knife, then add them whole to whatever I am cooking. The garlic cloves can then be removed before puréeing or serving so that food is gently flavoured rather than overpowered by the garlic.

JULIENNE: a term used to describe a vegetable or fruit that has been sliced into very fine, even strips

JUS: a concentrated stock made by roasting the bones of an animal then simmering them with water, aromatics and vegetables and reducing the resulting liquid. See pages 17-18 for recipes.

MIREPOIX: equal amounts of vegetables, diced to about 2-3 cm/^{3}/$_4$-1^1/$_4$ in long.

PARISIENNE SCOOPER: a small round scoop like a mini ice-cream scoop, used for shaping soft fruit, vegetables, chocolates, etc, into little balls.

PETALS: in the restaurant we often decorate a finished dish with deseeded tomatoes and peppers, cut into petal shapes. To make tomato petals, blanch the tomatoes first in boiling salted water for 2 minutes, then peel them. Cut the flesh vertically into 4 even strips and remove the seeds.

TO SAUTÉ: to cook an ingredient briefly in hot fat, turning it constantly so that it cooks quickly and evenly.

TO TURN POTATOES: use a sharp knife to shape peeled potatoes into six-sided barrels or cylinders. This helps make a dish look neat and professional, but is not essential.

VINAIGRETTE: an emulsification of olive oil with vinegar, salt and pepper made up of 3 parts oil to 1 part vinegar. Whisk the vinegar with the salt and pepper until the salt has dissolved, then add the olive oil and whisk again to emulsify.

Tabletop products shown in photographs: Leather backgrounds and accessories available from:
Alma Home, Unit D, 12-14 Great Orex Street, London E1 5NF
Tel: 020 7377 0762

Mach & Garbarino,
43 Kilmaine Road,
London SW6 7JU
Tel: 020 7610 0855

China and accessories from:
Bodo Sperlein, Unit 1,
12 OXO Tower Wharf, Barge House Street, London SE1 9PH
Tel: 020 7633 9413

Jhan Stanley,
27 Queen Street, Castlefields, Shrewsbury SY1 2JX
Tel: 01743 351 549

The Conran Shop,
Michelin House,
81 Fulham Road,
London SW3 6RD
Tel: 020 7589 7401

Heal's,
196 Tottenham Court Road,
London W1 9LD
Tel: 020 7636 1666

All other items hired

Index

Index